MW00885057

# LOVE WINS
## ENNIS, MONTANA

### A TRUE STORY OF TRAGEDY, HEROES, AND HEALING IN A SMALL TOWN

KAREN WATSON MCMULLIN

## Testimonials for Karen Watson McMullin and *Love Wins*

As the former mayor of a small town and past member of a volunteer fire department, this book was very reminiscent and illustrative of the tide of emotions both jobs presented to me. I was riveted from the moment I began reading this story and was barely conscious of a tortuous delayed airline flight. That inconvenience granted me the privilege to read it without interruption.

**-Sherry J. Scott, Former Mayor of Waycross, Georgia; former member of Pierce County Volunteer Fire Department, Blackshear, Georgia**

An eye-opening account of small-town unity in the face of big-time tragedy, this narrative interweaves stories of reaction and resilience, stasis and growth, demonstrating the potential we all share to rise to the occasion—together.

**-K. Shimkin, Nationally Registered Advanced-EMT (NRAEMT); Ohio**

In a world where breaking news headlines exploit tragedy, brutalize survivors, and highlight the villains, this story pays a beautiful tribute to heroes: everyday people who did what they could to love their neighbors when tragedy struck.

**-Simeon Morell, Law enforcement officer, SWAT team member; Wisconsin**

This story, of course, must be told, and not just for those who may still harbor a false sense of security in rural communities, nor only for the sake of the survivors of one of modern Montana's most shocking crimes. It's a story we all need to hear throughout the United States today.

The power of this story comes from its voice. McMullin speaks from within the still beating heart of the Ennis community as one of its own, the only practicing attorney in Ennis for almost three decades. Now, over twenty years later, she unsparingly reveals the exact details of the crime: seven young adults shot at an impromptu June reunion outside an Ennis bar; one deceased, several critically wounded; assailant wounds Florence deputy, then is shot in dramatic stop on Lolo Pass.

More than that, through countless interviews, she reveals the inside thoughts and courageous recovery of the decedent's family and the survivors, through the love of the whole dang town---not just the frothy, emotional stuff, but the apple crisp, fund at the local banks, cards and visits, phone calls five years later kind of love. Because when you have such a community, love does win, no matter what.

**-Roberta Zenker, County Attorney of Madison County, Montana, from 1997 to 2006**

Copyright © 2024 by Karen Watson McMullin.

All rights reserved. No part of this book may be reproduced in whole or in part without written permission from the publisher or author, except by reviewers who may quote brief excerpts in connection with a review in a newspaper, magazine, or electronic publication; nor may any part of this book be reproduced, stored in a retrieval system, or transmitted in any form or by any means electronic, mechanical, photocopying, recording, or other, without written permission from the publisher or author.

Karen Watson McMullin/Love Wins
Printed in the United States of America

Although every precaution has been taken to verify the accuracy of the information contained herein, the author and publisher assume no responsibility for any errors or omissions. No liability is assumed for damages that may result from the use of information contained within.

Love Wins/ Karen Watson McMullin -- 1st ed.

ISBN 9798339184584 Print Edition

# Contents

*Damn, it's beautiful here. Almost as though the creator was imbedded into the landscape. If Mother Earth were a symphony and God its composer, then it was the heavens he chose to orchestrate this place.*

—From the journal of Gavin Faulkner, June 13, 2003
Ennis High School Class of 2002

Jamie L. Roberts

# Introduction

## *Our Own Eden*

In early summer 2003, small communities like Ennis, Montana radiate a sense of unity, a renewed appreciation for familiar faces in day-to-day life. People are more likely to meet eyes warmly, in recognition of what is no longer taken for granted. The September 11 attacks happened barely two years before. Since then, the U.S. and NATO allies have invaded Afghanistan and then Iraq; armed undercover "sky marshals" are a frequent presence on civilian flights to prevent further terrorist attacks; and now a former U.S. army sergeant is awaiting trial, accused of committing the Washington, D.C. sniper shootings. The world "out there" is nonsensical and terrifying.

But life in Ennis, population 864, feels safe, and its citizens are aware of that. They're grateful. At least horrors like that don't happen here. The awful scenes on the evening news have aroused a heightened awareness of what really matters in life: *Focus on the little things you can change in this world and take particularly good care of your family and neighbors.* The conversations among the patrons in the Ennis Cafe resound with gratitude to live in a place where national-newsworthy happenings are profoundly unlikely. The morning regulars sit in their usual seats, have their usual breakfasts, and greet other

1

regulars—who are all familiar. This is a comfort, an assurance of a predictable future.

The storefronts here are charmingly Western, a theme maintained for many generations and upheld with artistry and pride. The front of the Ennis Cafe displays a beautiful mural of a pack train: a stately cowboy leading three pack horses through deep timber. Above them, in quiet reverie among the pine trees, stands a regal elk. Hanging above a tackle shop is an artist's rendition of the largest fly-fishing fly ever made. Each and every storefront has been well maintained and pays similar respect to the valley's dual reputation for outdoor recreation and Old West ranch life.

The stupendous views from east to west in the Madison Valley change with the light and seasons and never cease to amaze. Walking down Main Street one sees the flag flying at the Veterans Memorial, spectacular mountain ranges in the distance, and a world-renowned trout-fishing river. It's that beautiful here.

Strangers come through the Madison Valley every summer seeking a return to its "stand still" kind of life, where ranching still reigns; the first day of hunting season is as big a deal as Christmas, big trout stories are meant to be told for years, and everyone waves to oncoming vehicles because they probably do know the other drivers. Many visitors also realize that this remote-feeling place is connected to their own home, because rivers have a way of connecting us all. Winding its way out of Yellowstone National Park, the Madison River courses through the wide Madison Valley, and then it joins the Jefferson and Gallatin Rivers at Three Forks, Montana, forming the headwaters of the Missouri River.

The summer visitors bring their big-city pocketbooks and spend happily at the bars, restaurants, and motels, and pay their fishing guides well. All this pours into the bank accounts of countless small-business owners and feeds the families who live here year-round. The population of the Madison Valley increases in the summers, and there are jobs created overnight, aligning perfectly with the return of the valley's youth from far-flung colleges and universities.

Ennis has had a population hovering around 1,000 for many years. The town borders encompass approximately one square mile, and it sits at an elevation of approximately 4,900 feet. Winters are long in duration and short on daylight. Temperatures regularly fall into the teens and well below zero when windchill is considered. This kind of winter simplifies life and expectations.

High school sports consume everyone's attention. Everyone knows how the football, basketball, and volleyball teams are doing, and if there is a big game on a dark November night, the lights will be blazing at the football field. Most businesses close, except those that feed the crowds arriving with the opposing team. Most of the Ennis residents can be found bundled up in the bleachers or pacing the sidelines.

Basketball season begins just before the holidays and follows through the coldest winter months. The gym is packed from after-noon until night, with the earliest games played by the shortest little stick figures, apt to miss every basket. But even they are cheered by riotously engaged and vocal fans pounding on the bleachers in support, triumph, and frustration.

School buses travel hundreds of miles during the two seasons. Drivers make those trips numerous times, giving up their weekend evenings and providing their heartfelt support for their team. Following close behind each bus is a fleet of vehicles full of parents and other fans, dedicated to seeing games hours away, over wintry, snow-covered roads.

Spring is whimsical, with one foot in, one foot out. Early flowers bloom one day and are covered by three inches of snow the next. The lengthening days and welcome sunlight warm the ground, which soon sprouts miles of green grass—only to be hidden, yet again, under heavy wet snow.

Ranching is a hallmark of life in the Madison Valley. Some ranches in the valley have a history of 100 years or more. While ownership may have changed, the lives of the families engaged in each operation have not. The conditions in the valley are not overly favorable for ranching. The length of winters and the "Chinook" wind, which comes up frequently, are significant complications. Life here is not easy. Cows must be fed if there is snow on the ground, no matter the weather conditions. Calves are often born in the deepest, darkest, coldest days of winter, and the rancher attends to them, no matter the hour. Summer brings the duties of moving cattle, irrigating, cutting grass and hay, and repairing and maintaining all the infrastructure that makes ranching possible.

The young people who grow up in the Madison Valley, and attend school in Ennis, enjoy small classes. In the early 2000s, there is still just one class group for each grade. Kids here often go to school with the same 30 or so peers throughout their entire education. They grow up knowing each other, from the kindergarten sandbox to the high school football field, and they are all well acquainted with their friends' parents and extended families.

This small town is, itself, one big extended family that's proud of being so close-knit. The town also prides itself in being a welcoming host to outsiders. Every summer an annual Fourth of July Parade and Rodeo, hosted by the Ennis Chamber of Commerce and Ennis Rodeo Association, brings tens of thousands of visitors. The businesses and the Ennis Lion's Club volunteers manage to feed and meet all the needs of those visitors for one happy chaotic summer day. There is jubilant expectation for that event every year. It is no different in 2003.

Plans and excitement certainly begin to build in June. Everyone is in good spirits, of course, because of the return of long daylight hours and the snowpack melting into all of the valley's creeks, which flood into the Madison River. Spring's deep rich green blanket of grass now climbs up from the valley floor, along the foothills, and up to the highest mountain conifers. Dawn comes before most are ready to rise, and fades to sunset noticeably later each day, restoring youthful energy to all the inhabitants. Being located at 45 degrees north, it is light until nearly 10:00 p.m. at the summer solstice.

Mid-June 2003 abounds with hopeful anticipation of long warm days filled with outdoor enjoyment and gregarious family gatherings. Favorite mountain trails and lakes, inaccessible all winter, are finally thawing out and opening up for hiking, camping, and of course, fishing. One may fish in remote trout streams high up in the mountain ranges, as well as in the beloved Madison River right at the edge of town.

June is a wondrous month in the Madison Valley for one more reason. So many college-aged youth enroll in either the state universities and colleges in bigger Montana towns, or they head to schools in other states entirely. In June, they all come home. They take summer jobs on ranches, moving irrigation pipe and cows, or they work as wait staff at the many restaurants that need to "staff up" for the impending tourist season, or they work in the few motels that operate only during the summer.

The streets are already bustling. Travelers are eager to enjoy a meal at a cafe that embodies the essence of casual American dining, with red leather booths and white coffee cups, which are continually filled. They park along Main Street and venture into shops full of boutique Western goods, which will be generously bestowed upon any unfortunates remaining at home. Tourists file in to share drinks at any of a number of historical, vividly Western bars. Genuine cowboys have leaned against those same bars for more than a century, and those cowboys and cowgirls are still omnipresent.

The largest operating cattle ranch in the Madison Valley is the Bar 7. It has historical relevance as the location for *Golden Fleece,* written by Hughie Dickinson Call. The author came to the Madison Valley and, in 1920, lived at what is now the Bar 7 Ranch. She wrote in great detail of her life there, back when it was a sheep ranch. In 2003, that ranch is owned by a family who came to the valley from Nebraska, and it is a large and admirable operation.

The ranch manager is Arnie Rosdahl, who has managed the Bar 7 for 12 years. As the summer begins, like all ranch managers, he scouts for seasonal help for the immense acreage under his care. Mr. Rosdahl receives an application from the local Job Service Office from a man named George Harold Davis. Since the references check out, Davis is hired. Not a soul knows that, in this moment, a crack forms in our town's rock-solid foundation. This terrible fracture, as yet undetected, will challenge, shake, and shift Ennis, Montana for months and years to come.

*When I despair, I remember that all through history the way of truth and love have always won. There have been tyrants and murderers, and for a time, they can seem invincible, but in the end, they will always fall. Think of it—always.*

—Mahatma Gandhi

# Chapter 1

## *The Promise*

GAVIN FAULKNER, Ennis High School Class of 2002

June 13, 2003 is one month before Gavin Faulkner's nineteenth birthday. A friendly and cheerful, sun-blond young man with a chiseled jaw, Gavin is back from attending the University of Montana in Missoula for his freshman year. Although he had a wonderful first year and made new friends, he is elated to be home for the summer with his family, his old friends, his brother, Garrett, the town of Ennis, and the Madison Valley.

Gavin's family moved to Ennis, Montana from California, several years earlier. His mother, Maggi, moved there to be with her husband, J. T. France, the son of Ennis icon Johnny France. When Gavin came to Ennis, folks didn't know him, but they knew his stepfather's lineage. Shirttail relative or not, the story of Johnny France was now part of the new boy's heritage as well.

In 1986, Johnny France, then Sheriff of Madison County, single-handedly captured and arrested the father and son "Mountain Men" outlaws, Don and Dan Nichols. The two had attempted to kidnap a young female Montana State University student who was jogging on a trail in Big Sky. They planned to force her to live in the mountains with them. Instead, they murdered one of her would-be rescuers and shot the young woman in the chest. Don and Dan Nichols escaped into the mountains above Ennis. The men had been the subjects of a two-county manhunt for eight months, when Johnny France walked into their hidden mountain camp on an icy, early morning and single-handedly captured them. After an expeditious Montana trial, both father and son began long prison sentences in the State Prison at Deer Lodge.

This story, no doubt, transferred some weight of expectation onto Gavin's shoulders. He now carried countless unspoken responsibilities for how he would comport himself as a member of this family in this small town, now his adopted home since he was a young teen. But this Friday evening, Gavin's thoughts are far from all that. This is the first weekend of the summer that all his friends from high school are back from far-flung colleges and universities. Everyone is planning get-togethers. It's time to reconnect, and Gavin can't wait.

He lights up the telephone lines—mostly landlines, since not everyone has cell phones in this valley yet. He makes plans with Andrea—a cute girl he likes—and another high school friend, Trett Sutter. There is a popular local band playing at the Wells Fargo Steakhouse in Virginia City, a historic mining town 14 miles from Ennis. The trio decide to meet in downtown Ennis and carpool over to Virginia City.

TRETT SUTTER, Ennis High School Class of 2004

Trett Sutter is a serious, broodingly handsome young man, and his summer job has already begun, working with a local wood flooring company owned by his uncle, Bart Nestegard. One week into this physically demanding job, he is happy to hear from Gavin about tonight's proposed plans.

They meet Andrea in town and pile into Gavin's car. The three friends chatter away during the 15-minute ride over the Virginia City Pass, sharing news and stories about the past year since they've last seen one another. Trett, who is typically more quiet, appreciates his extroverted friend, Gavin—the type of guy who keeps a conversation going and is tuned in to the successes and joys of others. Gavin is clearly eager to hear how both Andrea and Trett have gotten along in the previous year. The three speak of mutual friends, summer plans, and shared joy.

When they get to Virginia City, they enter the bar at the Wells Fargo Steakhouse and find many more acquaintances and friends. They greet and are warmly enveloped by a familiar crowd. They stand and chat a while, then find seats. The Andrew Gromiller Band from McAllister, Montana begins to play songs reminiscing about glorious past memories. Trett watches Gavin get up to find a dance partner. Gavin sees his mom's good friend, Kelly Kivlin, a red-haired beauty and the hostess of the restaurant, and asks her to dance. That's Gavin. He can make friends with anyone, of any age, bringing the best out of them all.

A melodic and ethereal rendition of Norah Jones' "Come Away with Me" laces itself into the cool night air, drifting through the open windows and door. The room abounds with warmth and friendship. Gavin tips his head back and looks around the room at Kelly and at this circle of friends and extended family. Much later, he'll say of that moment that he felt "totally at peace."

ISAIAH CROWLEY, Ennis High School Class of 2000

Another group of friends, Isaiah Crowley, Matthew Ortega (Class of 1999), and Jake Stewart (Class of 2000), all get together in downtown Ennis for a quick beer. Then this trio also heads "over the hill" to hear the popular local band and start their evening at the Wells Fargo Steakhouse. They plan to return to Ennis for more socializing after the band finishes.

Isaiah Crowley is a gentle 22-year-old, soft-spoken man, with earnest eyes and a construction worker's strong build. He moved to Ennis several years earlier. He first lived with Brad Bullock, and now lives with Shorty Roberts and Jaime Singleton Roberts, whom he calls his "Ennis mom and dad."

Isaiah works for Singleton Construction, owned by Jaime's father, Jim Singleton, and managed by Brad Bullock. So go the connections in a town this small; everyone knows everyone, and most people own, or work at, one of several small businesses. Both Brad and Jim know what a valuable employee Isaiah is to the company. But, like all the adults who know him, these two mentors encourage Isaiah to continue in school. For his part, Isaiah has always had a feeling, even at a very early age, that the construction field will be his life's work.

Isaiah has essentially been on his own since he was fairly young. The town of Ennis became the family he always needed. Years earlier, with a home provided to him first by Brad and then Shorty and Jaime, Isaiah was able to work as much as he liked, while he returned to school to earn his high school diploma from Ennis High School, along with the class of 2000. He was a few years older than his classmates but surrounded by supportive adults and peers. Jaime, Isaiah's "Ennis mother," describes him as having the kindest, most loving heart and wittiest disposition. Jaime and Shorty have three other children close to Isaiah's age, and he is absorbed into their family through the love and grace so characteristic of their home.

Isaiah is mature beyond his years, and has engendered respect from his peers, both in his high school class and with his construction crew. He gets the invitation to go out this Friday evening and decides to accompany his friends, Jake Stewart and Matthew Ortega. He, too, is looking forward to hearing the Andrew Gromiller Band play at the Wells Fargo.

## MATTHEW ORTEGA, Ennis High School Class of 1999

As summer begins for Matthew, he is happy to hear from Isaiah and Jake about the plans for the evening. Matthew is a hardworking, tall, dark-eyed, dark-haired young man from a large family of sons, who have lived in the Madison Valley for several years. He, his parents, and many of his brothers are involved in the family's pivot irrigation installation business, Ortega & Sons, and they all attend the Ennis Assembly of God Church.

Matthew, Isaiah, and Jake meet at the Silver Dollar Saloon on Main Street in Ennis. They have a beer with Brad Bullock and another man, who is seated by Brad. They've never met this stranger. He is introduced as George Davis—a tall, slim, heavy-browed man with shy eyes, a straggly beard, and a ranch hand's Carhartt and denim garb. The conversation is casual, and no one thinks much of any of the words exchanged. All are friendly and relaxed.

Jake, Isaiah, and Matthew then take their leave and carpool together over the hill, for the 14-mile drive to Virginia City. The bar is packed when they arrive at the Wells Fargo. They see and greet Trett,

13

Gavin, and Andrea and then mingle. It takes plenty of time to touch base with everyone they know, as the place is brimming with friends and acquaintances from Ennis, both young and not-so-young and, of course, all the regulars from Virginia City. A tight ring of always-engaging familiarity, trust, and jocularity draws everyone together. The band plays songs that make the old wistful, and the young hopeful. The light wanes as the full moon rises. The music carries everyone; it is a perfect summer moment, a place full of life and joy.

## GAVIN FAULKNER

Gavin, Trett, and Andrea soon decide to leave. Gavin, being 18 years old and sober, is happy to serve as designated driver, taking Andrea and Trett back over the Virginia City Hill to Ennis. They agree, along the way, to head to the Claim Jumper. Gavin is delighted as Brad and Kelly DiIorio, his aunt and uncle, own that bar and, in a way, he feels he does too.

When the friends enter, the place is packed. The horseshoe-shaped bar is the pivotal magnet for the large, jostling crowd. Barks of laughter and loud country music from the jukebox heighten all the patrons' senses. The pool table is the center of fierce though friendly competition, and passersby are careful to duck their heads to avoid pool cue injuries. All the tables are occupied, and the bar is several people deep in a wriggling mass of happy humanity.

People jostle, converse, and mingle, many making their way through the crowd with drinks held high. Brad and Kelly see Gavin, and warmly welcome their nephew and his friends. Gavin is elated to share "his family's bar" with these two friends and so many others he is so delighted to see again for the first time this summer. He surveys the crowd and approaches and greets all of his Ennis High School classmates with his natural "Gavin charm." The music is loud, the crowd is louder, and no one's glass is empty.

Then Gavin notices a man whose strangely forbidding presence stands out from all this summer joy. He approaches the man with his natural youthful optimism. Gavin is instinctively drawn to care for people, and this one strikes him as a person needing serious care. George Davis sits alone, and all movement around him seems held at bay by some carefully drawn force field. Gavin edges closer to the man, hoping to attempt some friendly conversation.

He simply asks, "How are you doing tonight?" This one innocuous question triggers a quick and angry rant of spewed racial hatred. Gavin is taken aback but continues to try to converse with the man for a moment. Other than those initial ugly words, George Davis has little else to say. This is like dark meeting light, warm meeting cold. The man's darkness chills Gavin but does not erode his natural kindness. When the man meets Gavin's persistent warmth with a scowl and little else, Gavin takes his leave and thinks: *Now there's a man who needs a fucking hug.* He considers warning his friends but sees that they are all happily engaged in warm and pleasant conversations elsewhere.


BRAD DIIORIO, Owner of The Claim Jumper

At the same time, Brad DiIorio, Gavin's uncle and the bar owner, also becomes aware of George Davis and his sinister essence and bearing. The other patrons are clearly affected by this guy. Brad watches the encounter with his nephew and sees the effect that George Davis has on Gavin. Soon after that, Brad decides that he's had his fill of this man, and he takes the liberty granted to bar owners the world over.

Brad approaches George Davis and has a brief exchange with him. Brad does not like how the guy responds to his questions. A big man himself, he efficiently grabs George Davis by the front of his shirt, lifts him from his seat, and physically ejects him from the Claim Jumper, onto the sidewalk outside. Brad easily dispels the lanky ranch hand. The bar owner may have been rough, but none would declare his actions to be wrongful. George Davis, now head down and shuffling, makes his miserable way further west, towards the Silver Dollar Bar.

Shortly thereafter, Gavin, Andrea, and Trett also leave the Claim Jumper. Unwittingly, they follow George Davis down to the Silver Dollar. It is getting late, almost closing time.

## JASON KLAUMANN, Ennis High School Class of 1996

Jason is a powerfully built young man with a kind countenance. He attended Montana Technical Institute in Butte after graduation and obtained an engineering degree, which gave him excellent and immediate employment in Salt Lake City. He has many responsibilities for his young age. This trip home is a nice break from all those work-related demands. He's here to attend a friend's bachelor party scheduled for the next day, Saturday, June 14. This Friday night feels like a pre-party of sorts.

Jason's soon-to-be-wife, Beth Toivonen, drove with him from Salt Lake and dropped him off at his family's home in Ennis. She then drove on to Dillon to be with her own family for the weekend. As Jason arrives in Ennis on Friday evening, he stops in to say hello to his parents, Stan and Martha Klaumann, and then he heads down to the Silver Dollar to see if any of his friends are there.

He knows everyone in the bar with few exceptions, and he's happy to see Mike Carroll, Gavin Faulkner, and Trett Sutter. Although younger than him, Jason knows them because his younger sisters went to Ennis High School with them. He also greets three female friends: Angie Hoe (Kujula), Ginger Powers (Nelson), and Nicole Toppel (Gribbons). They're sitting at a table by themselves. The three make for a noticeably lovely breath of feminine energy in the bar. Everyone visits and catches up, enjoying the evening surrounded by friends and warm interactions amongst familiar, longtime acquaintances.

## MIKE CARROLL, GINGER POWERS (NELSON), ANGIE HOE (KUJULA), NICOLE TOPPEL (GRIBBONS); all Ennis High School Class of 1998

By day, Mike Carroll works in construction for Dan Milliken and Tom Savage. Mike graduated with Ginger, and they have been a couple since high school, planning to marry soon. Their son Cameron's fifth birthday was June 11, just two days ago. Mike is a handsome, easy-going young man, liked by all, and he's happy to join his many friends for this festive summer evening.

Ginger Powers is a gentle, soft-spoken, dark-haired, luminously beautiful young woman with many responsibilities for her young age. She, like Mike, works hard. During the days, she helps friends with the care of their young children while she cares for their own son, Cameron, and in the evenings, she works as a waitress at the Ennis Bowling Alley.

Angie Hoe is one of three dark-haired, brown-eyed, beautiful sisters. She is delighted when her dear friends, Nicole and Ginger arrange to belatedly celebrate her college graduation. Angie graduated from Montana State University and now lives in Bozeman, working at First Security Bank. Her parents, Tim and Rene Hoe, live in McAllister. Angie's trip back to the Madison Valley is a chance for her to visit her parents as well.

Nicole Toppel is an athletic, tan, blonde woman who attends Lynn University in Boca Raton, Florida. As usual, she is home for the summer. Her parents, Dennis and Charlotte Toppel, live up South Meadow Creek in McAllister. Nicole has been looking forward to this get-together with her two best friends.

The three women meet at the Silver Dollar Saloon, claim a free table, and enjoy catching up, their beautiful heads tipped closely together. They see many people they know, including Andrea who comes in with Gavin and Trett. Andrea has been living in Ennis for several months with extended family. She is close to the three women sitting at the table. They quickly reconnect.

While the young women chat at their own table, many of their male friends stand nearby. These include Ginger's fiancé, Mike Carroll. The young men have put in a day of hard work or have just returned from college. All look forward to summer jobs and outdoor adventures in their home valley.

Like the Claim Jumper, the Silver Dollar is also packed, with every bar stool and table now occupied and people standing five deep at the bar. The shellacked wooden bar runs the entire distance all along the west side of the establishment. The mirror, which sits over the bar back, helps patrons survey the room and sight old friends. The compulsory pool table is in full action with an amiable waiting list, even though closing time is not too far off. Bar patrons continue to mingle and greet one another, with a warmth and kindness that is typical on any evening in Ennis, but particularly so, with so many of the town's youth now home. The faces reflected in the grand mirror make up a star-studded collection of Ennis High School graduates. Some are in college. Others are older; they've graduated and are working and living life back in their hometown. The thread that connects them all, from kindergarten through high school, is palpable.

Most in the crowd naturally mill about, but there is one man who seems solely transfixed by the table of young women—Ginger, Angie, Nicole, and Andrea. George Davis begins to jockey through the crowd to get close to their table. He tries to get their attention, tries to engage them in conversation, but his loud entreaties are bizarre and repugnant: *I'm 45 and I like young girls… I am a 45-year-old pervert.* Other sickening missives only repulse the young women. Their friends begin to overhear the verbal harassment.

The women tell George Davis, more than once, that they have no interest in him. No harsh or angry words are spoken. But the women are firm. This doesn't dissuade George Davis; he keeps at them. A few young men nearby hear him and become highly alarmed. They circle closer, working through the crowd to place their bodies between George Davis and their female friends.

## JAMIE L. ROBERTS, Ennis High School Class of 1994

Jamie was two years old when he came to Ennis, Montana with his mother, Sharon. She later married a local man, Doug Clark. Jamie was raised by his mother and Doug, to become the young man he is now: husband to Kandi; father of a young daughter, Kyra; secretary of the Bowling League; member of the Madison Valley Rural Fire Department; and a full-time, valued employee of MDM

Construction Company, owned by Mike and Cindy McKitrick. He works hard, takes care of his family, is involved in the community, and is beloved by an immense circle of friends and townspeople.

Jamie seems to always be where the fun is. His broad smile and coltish good looks make him popular and magnetic. He's easy to talk to, and many seek out his company and conversation on this night. Gregarious and funny, tonight he especially enjoys being amongst his friends and with his father, Doug.

Jamie knows everyone in the bar, and as he surveils the room, he takes note of George Davis and his awkward attempts to interact with the table of girlfriends. Jamie is someone who always has his eyes open for those left out of the group—as well as those who may be a threat to the group. He is one of several men who note that George Davis may need corralling. Jamie tries to maneuver the man away from the young women.

For a time, the young men in the community successfully buy the women some space. The girlfriends are able to resume their catching-up conversation, surrounded by Mike, Jamie, and other well-known guy friends. But everyone's blissful evening is changing, the mood slightly tainted by this stranger, who is dressed like a ranch hand but acts like none of the ranchers they know so well.

Mike Carroll, Jake Stewart, Gavin Faulkner, Trett Sutter, Jason Klaumann, and Jamie Roberts realize that George Davis is getting louder and more aggressive, still trying to verbally assault the young women. They all try to corral him away. Jason even tries to buy

George Davis a drink. Gavin tries, again, to engage him in conversation, trying to "get the essence of the man" and "take the edge off" him. Jamie intervenes, yet again, simply trying to divert the man's attention away from the young women.

The young men watch hopelessly as they witness George Davis successfully wedge his way through the crowd once more, reach behind the back of Andrea's shoulder, and touch her in an attempt at an unasked-for massage. The atmosphere quickens and eyes meet. Everyone sees Andrea's sharp, negative, and repulsed reaction. At the searing touch of his hand, Andrea stands up hastily, nearly knocking over her heavy wooden chair. She turns sharply away and asks Nicole to give her a ride home, a request that Nicole hastily honors. The two depart. There is a collective exhalation when they are safely out the door, and everyone hears the sound of Nicole's Jeep backing out. A momentary calm returns. Still, a hot molten hostility now swirls amongst all these youthful hearts. There is some self-preserving sense awakening in them. The entire group is on alert.

A few minutes later, Jason Klaumann watches as George Davis makes his way to leave the bar. In all appearances, it seems he may not pay his bar tab. Jason's good friend, Laura Clark (Laura Clark [Helling], Class of 1998), is the bartender. Jason knows that if the man fails to pay his tab, Laura will have to pay for it out of her own meager wages, as is the custom in this business. This disturbs Jason. As George Davis has already gone out and come back once, and still not paid, Jason is getting concerned. He has a deep-seated sense of propriety, and he cannot understand how this man could consider leaving a bartender in the lurch.

Jason hears his friends making plans to go to Jamie Roberts' house after the bar closes. He is watching Laura clean up and wants her to be able to go with them. He knows that she won't be able to leave until George Davis settles his bill. Jason sees the man leave once more and hopes that means that he is finally getting money out of his car, parked on Main Street.

It is now minutes to closing time, and Jamie finishes inviting all the young people to come to his home. He makes sure everyone knows the plan, then he leaves the bar, checking on Laura with a backward glance. *Does she need any help with closing?* She shakes her head in a universal "I'm okay." Jamie heads up Main Street to gather others to attend the spontaneous after-party at his house.

Gavin and Trett finish their pool game and settle their tab. They head outside onto Main Street. The moon is full, it's easy to see, and they recognize other friends, whom they'd seen earlier back at Virginia City: Jake Stewart, Matthew Ortega, and Isaiah Crowley.

An expectant milling-about pours out of the bars and onto the sidewalks along Main Street. Friends convene in shadowy groups; occasional laughter erupts above the quiet din of conversation. The full moon is bright enough to cast shadows, and there is a slight breeze. The evening is still full of friends and good cheer and expectations. As the moon arcs slowly overhead, its light dappling through the trees, the young people can almost hear the whisper of summer's promise.

Several friends stand talking outside the bank. They form a circle, but not a closed ring, and this group would likely welcome any and all who would care to join. Another group is forming at the doorway of the Silver Dollar.

Mike and Ginger are still in the Silver Dollar, quietly chatting about calling it a night and heading back to their empty mobile home; they are so appreciative of Ginger's mother and father who are caring for five-year-old Cameron for the night at their place in the Upper Ruby Valley. The couple also chats with Doug Clark, Jamie Roberts' father. Nicole, who returned to the bar after dropping off Andrea, is with Angie. The two women are just behind Mike and Ginger, gathering their things. They push back the heavy wooden chairs with a scrape and thud, a sound that reverberates through the almost-empty bar, signaling the end of the evening.

# Chapter 2

## *The Breach*

J ust before 2:00 a.m., official closing-time calls reverberate around those still inside the bars. Laura Clark continues with all her usual tasks, cleaning and closing down the bar for the day. Jamie Roberts is already up the street inviting any other friends exiting from the Claim Jumper to come over to his house. He's trying, with all his youthful delight, to keep the fun from ending.

The full moon glows above, and soft chatter and bursts of laughter cascade down the street. In stark contrast, George Davis wanders just outside the bar, looking sullen and brooding. He passes right by Jason Klaumann, who is polite but direct when he asks the man to settle his bar tab with Laura. Jason explains that she will have to cover his unpaid bill from her own salary if he does not pay it himself. George Davis has been drinking the entire evening, and Jason knows this tab could significantly dent Laura's wages.

Jason watches as George Davis continues on to his car and, instead of reaching in to grab a wallet, the man simply gets in and drives off. Jason thinks to himself: *Well, that settles that. Not in a good way, but so be it. At least that malevolent presence is gone.*

Jason notices two larger clusters of people outside. There's a circle of young men, friends who have reconnected after seeing each other earlier in Virginia City. Another smaller group of young people spills out from the Silver Dollar, mostly on the steps, just at the entrance. Others are getting in their cars. Engines start, and many begin the drive home. A few duos and trios continue both whispered and exuberant conversations in the moonlit summer stillness.

Suddenly, Jason is startled to see George Davis return, parking his older Ford Taurus in front of the Ennis Pharmacy just up the street and west of the Silver Dollar. Jason is not at all happy to see him again, and his senses are on high alert as the man gets out of his car. Jason no longer hears the continued conversations around him. He focuses solely on Davis, as the man crosses the street to the front of the Long Branch Saloon, then immediately turns east, walking straight for the people who are still socializing just outside the bars.

Davis takes long, purposeful strides, right towards Jason. Angie, who is standing near Jason, sees the man too. She has the instinctive feeling to hide her face, pulling her hood up over her head. Though fighting their sense of repulsion toward this character, both Angie and Jason hail him and, once again, politely ask him to go back inside and pay his tab. They're feeling for Laura and just want her to be able to close up the bar and join everyone for the after-party at Jamie's.

Davis does go back in the bar, but only to briskly yell at Laura that he will "catch her tomorrow." Laura shakes her head with a frown and continues wiping down the bar. Angie goes back inside the Silver Dollar to connect with friends who are getting ready to leave. Meanwhile, Jason watches Davis as he once again leaves the bar and walks east down the sidewalk towards the group consisting of Matthew Ortega, Isaiah Crowley, Jake Stewart, Gavin Faulkner, and Trett Sutter. They are all standing next to Matthew's Volkswagen van. Jake's pickup is parked to the east of the van. The men are bunched together in a tight-knit group, talking, beneath the glow of a vapor streetlight.

Matthew and Isaiah turn, recognize the ranch hand from the Bar 7, whom they were introduced to much earlier in the evening. They greet Davis with smiles as he walks towards them. As Davis reaches their group, Matthew calls out, "Have a good evening!" The man does not even acknowledge that he heard Matthew. His head is down, and Matthew fleetingly feels sorry for him; he seems so heavy and sullen.

None of these young men are surprised or alarmed when the ranch hand fails to answer. Even the men who witnessed Davis's ugly behavior in the bar try to summon some sense of human compassion. Even now, if this man had walked up to the group and sincerely apologized for his earlier behavior, they might have accepted that apology and drawn him into their conversation. People around here are just that willing to give a broken man a second chance.

But it seems that Davis is going to pass right on by, continuing his lonely walk down the street. Although the group continues with its conversation, at that moment, Jake loses the thread; his entire focus is on this dark figure, seemingly retreating, but not yet far enough away for Jake to feel comfortable. Jake, like Jason, has been closely watching the man's behavior all evening.

Jake and Jason now have their eyes and full attention on Davis as the man continues several more paces, past the group. Jake turns partially away from his friends, to allow full sight of the man, who has sounded more internal alarms in Jake than he has ever experienced in his young life. As Jake turns, he has unwittingly put himself outside the safety net of the group.

Jason also watches Davis, from an unobstructed vantage point on the sidewalk just outside the Silver Dollar. Although they are not standing together, both Jake and Jason see clearly as Davis whirls around, reaches inside the front of his jacket with his right hand, then forcefully brandishes a .45 caliber semi-automatic pistol. Its barrel glints under both the full moon and the streetlight, gleaming with a horrific intensity that burns into each young man's consciousness.

Jake sees Davis hunch into a military-style triangle shooting stance, pointing the pistol directly at him. Jake is no stranger to weapons, having grown up in Montana hunting culture. Yet having a gun pointed directly at him from just ten feet away is beyond anything his life has prepared him for. Still, Jake doesn't freeze or panic. He instantaneously dodges and shouts, and the bullet aimed at him, miraculously, misses. In less than a heartbeat, Jake bolts away down the street.

There is nothing yet, but stillness; time feels frozen. All friendly conversations cease. The street is completely silent. Muscles brace, but none can grasp what in the world has just happened and what they should do next.

The horror that follows takes mere seconds. Davis turns several degrees, points and aims again. This time, at Isaiah Crowley. Isaiah's strong young body takes four bullets and drops onto the cold pavement. Beyond the reach of the most evil imagination, Davis pivots slightly, aims again, and shoots Gavin Faulkner in both his hand and right leg. Again, the predator pivots and aims. He shoots Trett Sutter in the right thigh.

Matthew Ortega, the one young man still standing in this group, is in shock, trying to make sense of what has happened, trying to grasp what he has just witnessed. Davis pivots again and shoots Matthew in the stomach. But Matthew does not go down. His survival instinct and strong will propel his wounded body into a mad dash for what he perceives to be safety. In a state of total shock, he runs across Main Street past the Ennis Pharmacy and into the alley behind that building.

The entire circle of young men has been fired upon, one by one. Yet comprehension has not caught up to this timeline of insanity. No one shot at has yet grasped the reality of the situation. No human experience has provided these young people with a framework for this nightmare.

Gavin, severely wounded, has taken flight on foot in a tight circle around the truck and then east, up the middle of Main Street. He leaves a trail of blood behind him. Trett, in spite of his injury, runs in the same direction as Gavin. Then, in what felt like tortuous slow motion, Trett gets himself into his own vehicle parked further east on Main Street.

Jake, the first to be fired upon, has seen all four of his friends shot within seconds: Isaiah, Gavin, Trett, and Matthew. Physically unharmed, Jake is still crouched behind a pickup and watching Davis through the cab's glass. When Davis has clearly emptied the magazine of his pistol, and the blasts momentarily cease, Jake knows he has a sliver of an opportunity for a getaway run. He catapults over the fence in front of Wild Rose Park and tears for the cover of other buildings and bushes.

Jason has seen everything too, and now in shock, sees Davis calmly eject the spent magazine, reach inside his jacket pocket, and pull out and insert another. Jason notices Jamie Roberts down the street. The young man had just finished casting his net to catch all his friends, inviting them to his after-party. He is now on the sidewalk in front of the Chamber of Commerce building. Jamie moves into the street, perhaps hearing the gunshots? *Has he caught on, is he about to run?* Jason can't tell. But before he can make sense of what's happening, Davis turns and sprints directly towards Jamie, closing the distance between them. Jamie is side-angled away from Davis, standing with his hands at his sides. He is calm and still, an expectant look on his young face. *No, Jamie has no idea what's happening.* Davis approaches within five feet of Jamie and another blast leaves the chamber of the pistol. The bullet strikes Jamie in his left arm and passes straight through his body. Jamie drops to the pavement, hard.

Only minutes have passed, but it seems an eternity. Jason now watches with sheer frozen horror as the nightmare apparition jogs down Main Street directly towards him—and the rest of the closing-time crowd still flowing in and out of the doorway and porch of the Silver Dollar Saloon.

Angie and Nicole come outside on the steps of the Silver Dollar and approach Jason. "Is someone setting off fireworks?" Angie asks innocently. It's not uncommon in Ennis, so close to the Fourth of July. Nicole is right behind Angie and hears the question. Jason grabs both girls by their elbows and pushes them down and towards a parked vehicle nearby. "No!" he says to the startled women. "It's a gun, it's a gun! Get down, please, just get down!"

*Fireworks.* That innocent assumption explains why Jamie, and so many others who heard the blasts, had not run away. In getting the women to relative safety, Jason has finally been able to move and speak. He no longer feels frozen by terror, and he has fully disavowed both himself and his friends of any illusions. He saw, and will forever see, the silhouette of that gun, the flash of the muzzle. *They are under fire. Their friends are bleeding on the pavement.*

Jason has pushed Angie and Nicole behind Nicole's Jeep, which is parked right in front of the Silver Dollar. He places himself behind an adjacently parked vehicle, and his mind screams with the question: "What do I do now?"

Davis is now within a few strides of them, though his attention is directed toward the bar. At that moment, Ginger Powers and Mike Carroll step out of the Silver Dollar, calling out over their shoulders to friends still inside. Davis points his weapon, takes aim, and shoots Ginger twice at close range. She is shot through the hips and thigh and collapses onto the steps. Davis once more takes aim and shoots Mike in the stomach. Mike is blown backwards, into the arms of Doug Clark—the father of Jamie Roberts. Doug has no idea that his own son has also been felled by this monster.

From their hiding place behind the Jeep, Nicole and Angie see their friends, Mike and Ginger, whom they have lived with their whole lives, shot and crumpled on the ground. Ginger is close, almost within reach, lying on the steps, bleeding. Nicole looks at the mask masquerading as a face on Davis and cannot believe how he says nothing, shows absolutely no emotion.

Nicole and Angie huddle, silently and desperately, behind the Jeep. They are crouched low, trying surreptitiously to see Davis, yet keep themselves hidden. Then Davis points the gun directly at them through the soft, fabric top of the Jeep. It is the old game of cat-and-mouse, but this is a madman, and their lives are his prize. They are terrified not only for themselves, but for their friends, Mike and Ginger, lying so helplessly right in front of them.

Nicole and Angie continue to watch Davis through the window of the Jeep, while they quietly crawl in the opposite direction. He menacingly stalks them around the body of the vehicle. They continue their circular crawl across the rough gravel on the street, scraping their legs, yet they feel nothing but horror.

At that moment, Jason finds his voice once more. He stands and yells loudly at Davis—a guttural roar of no known English word. This successfully distracts Davis, breaking him out of his hunt. Jason's shout does more than that. It breaks Davis's focus entirely. The monster suddenly sprints in the direction of his own parked car, across Main Street in front of the Ennis Pharmacy.

Jason has seen this man gun down Gavin, Trett, Isaiah, Matthew, Jamie, Mike, and Ginger, and attempt to kill Angie and Nicole as well. *How was a single yell enough to stop this monster's momentum?* Adrenaline-fueled, Jason finds himself throttling and waving an empty beer bottle. He considers pursuing Davis to take him down. In his mind, he can feel the weight of the bottle impacting Davis's head or at least his shooting arm. But that thought is extinguished when Jason's legs absolutely cease to function, and he collapses, once more struggling to fight the weight of his shock. Seconds later, he finds himself seated on the pavement, gasping for air and control, in front of the Silver Dollar.

Jason, Angie, and Nicole see Davis speed away down Main Street to the west. But having left and returned once before, they cannot be certain of where he might go or what he will do next. Will he come back with more ammunition to continue his maniacal siege? The three young friends are utterly still for a moment. Impossibly, the moon is still shining, they are still breathing, and yet nothing, nothing is the same.

# Chapter 3

## *Torn*

Where tranquility and promise once reigned, there now lies a gaping breach. With what will that breach be filled? No community seeks out such a test of its very fiber. Yet here it is: *terror*. In that time after terror, a town must determine its future and the outcome of all those so intimately harmed.

There is no doubt that the forces of darkness do, too often, rend the delicate veil of human welfare. But neither can one doubt that, when this fabric is torn, many angels reside below to catch those who fall through.

The question is: *Does love win against such evil? Can it?*

# Chapter 4

## *Heroes*

In the wake of the rampage, Jason Klaumann is barely aware of what fuels his actions. Later he'll recall the many caring mentors in his past. Certainly, his father, Stan Klaumann, played a crucial role. He allowed Jason to accompany him in his duties as a longtime member of the Madison Valley First Responders and Ambulance Volunteers. His father also served as the Ennis town police officer for many years. There was also Coach Bob Cleverly, a man who believed first aid training was an essential component of the Government classes he taught for decades at Ennis High School. Then there was the more recent on-the-job training at Jason's Salt Lake City employer. There he learned about responding to serious emergency situations in the commercial construction setting.

The sum of all this training now serves as Jason's operating system for the rest of this awful night. It's surely the reason he functions so steadily, almost mechanically, instead of permanently freezing from fear and adrenaline. Jason sees a broken body in front of him, the body of a friend. He feels viscerally the potential deadly threat still at hand. But he shakes off that fear and is off to help the first person who seems the most harmed.

Jason gets to Jamie Roberts within minutes. He tries to position Jamie's upper body to begin CPR. But as he begins resuscitation, Jason immediately realizes that Jamie's chest cavity is full of blood. He knows he cannot help him. He feels a quiet presence at his side, and he lays his classmate and friend into the waiting arms of Jamie's father, Doug Clark. The man has sprinted to get there. He drops to the ground and begins doing CPR on his son himself. There is no time for Jason to process this: *his friend, his friend's father.* There are others in dire shape. Jason moves on.

He rushes through the entrance of the Silver Dollar, and learns that somehow, with super-human resolve, Doug had dragged Mike off the stoop and back inside—just before rushing out to look for his own son. Angie and Nicole had carried their friend Ginger inside. The two young women now hold Mike and Ginger in their arms. Jason leans down to apply pressure to Mike's abdominal wound with a piece of cloth he has in his hands. It's possible that cloth is from Jason's own shirt; only later will he become aware that he is shirtless.

Jason proceeds in this elevated state of adrenaline-fired activity. Unimpeded by any thought of his own vulnerability, he heads straight back outside, to help another victim. Even though everyone is uncertain of whether Davis will return.

Isaiah, who has taken four bullets (the most of anyone), is still on the street where he fell. Jason covers him with a blanket of some sort and applies pressure to the many wounds, then looks up as a familiar pickup truck skids to a stop next to him. The truck door flies open and Isaiah's Ennis father, Shorty Roberts, jumps out. Shorty too is shirtless, having rushed here straight out of bed after a terrible phone call. There is a moment, a confused glance between them. In ordinary circumstances the two men would surely share a nod and a chuckle—that they are both standing shirtless on Main Street in the mystery hours of the new morning. The horror at hand silences years of good-natured rapport.

Shorty takes over caring for Isaiah, which frees Jason to care for his other friends. Matthew is, unbelievably, still upright and dizzily walking around nearby. He ran from the scene briefly, but he's back now, and he is bleeding profusely through his red sweatshirt. Jason gently urges Matthew down to the ground and gets something to cover him. He then enlists an onlooker to apply pressure to Matthew's abdominal wound.

Seeing no other bodies nearby, Jason runs back inside the Silver Dollar and catapults himself over the bar to the phone. Laura already hit the panic button earlier, and the siren is piercing the scene with its own insistent wail, only adding to the sheer bedlam. But it's working, beckoning aid and assistance from townspeople living nearby. The police must be on the way, but seconds feel like hours. Jason wants to know for himself that they've been called.

First, he dials the Madison County Sheriff's Department Dispatch, and he tells the dispatcher everything he can possibly comprehend about the shooting—these are valuable eye-witness details that the police hadn't received yet. Jason doesn't stay on this call for long; he communicates enough to let dispatch know that they will need multiple ambulance transports and police reinforcements. Now. He then calls the cell phone of his father, Stan Klaumann, who lets him know he already got the page. He assures his son that he's already at the Ambulance Barn in the Ennis Town Hall; they're already gearing up for victim transport.

Jason tells his father everything that happened and specifically lists the names of the victims. Then he calls home and asks his mother, Martha Klaumann, to get over to Madison Valley Hospital. She is a longtime employee who has worked the switchboard there, and she and Jason agree that this very skill will be crucial right now.

In the minutes immediately following the shooting and his narrow escape, Trett Sutter drives wildly through the quiet back blocks of the town, his mind looping over and over what has just happened. He can't stop thinking of how close he was to Davis when the madman began shooting. It feels like no one reacted or moved soon enough, including himself. Even after several shots were fired, everyone still moved in slow motion.

His flight instinct certainly took over at some point, and he could not rationally recall anything more, except running to his car. He ran alongside Gavin for a while. The two veered in slightly different directions, and then Trett clamored into his car and sped off, not really yet aware of what had just happened.

He's coming to awareness now, driving around the familiar blocks. Trett, becoming more fully conscious, drives in the direction of Patti Sutter and Javier Ramirez's house, his mom and stepfather, who live over in the residential part of Ennis. On the way there, his mind begins to conquer the vise grip of physical and mental shock.

As he pulls up to the house, he reawakens to the fact that not only did he see friends drop to the ground, but he too has been hit. How does that begin to register? The pain in his thigh? The wet feel of his own blood on his hands? Perhaps it is the overhead light as he opens the car door. Whatever the case, this is the moment that he emerges into total awareness that he too was shot. He limps to the front door, opens it, and yells for his mom and Javier. They both come running with concern and dismay on their faces. Trett cannot initially articulate what has happened, and there is a moment of stillness as the three look at each other for some explanation. Action takes over, and Patti and Javier help Trett into their own vehicle. In hasty conversation, it is decided only Patti will take him to the hospital, leaving Javier with their younger sleeping child. Patti speeds the short distance across town, and Trett becomes the first of the wounded to arrive at Madison Valley Hospital.

Amazingly, Isaiah has been conscious this entire time, despite being hit by four bullets. He remembers how he saw Davis take aim. Isaiah yelled, and he believes that caused Davis to miss one of his shots. After Isaiah fell, he was still completely conscious as Davis proceeded down Main Street. He saw the man reload, saw Ginger get shot. Isaiah was also aware enough to realize that he had a cell phone with him. He managed to take it out and call Shorty, his Ennis dad.

Soon Isaiah is aware of people all around him, aware that he is on the ground, immobile. He is aware when someone, he's not sure who, tends to him and covers him. Then Shorty is at his side, within mere minutes. His Ennis dad loads him gently, with the ready assistance of a couple of bystanders, into his pickup truck. Isaiah is still aware and conscious as Shorty speeds off, rushing him to Madison Valley Hospital.

Matthew had actually seen the blast coming out of the gun. He'd stared in disbelief. He saw Isaiah fall and then saw the gun aim at him and felt the bullet going right through his torso. *How strange. It didn't hurt; it felt more like an internal tickle.* He felt his sweatshirt turn wet. But still, he wasn't certain that it was blood darkening his already red sweatshirt.

An unknown source of strength powered Matthew to run toward the alley behind the Ennis Pharmacy. The back street alley was empty and quiet—except for him flailing along. He reached the back of a shop building that had a side stairwell up to an apartment above. For no rational reason, he imprinted on that apartment door as a potential source of help and safety. He fumbled his way up the stairs. Matthew stood on the stoop, holding one hand against his bleeding abdomen and pounding on the door with his other fist. But no one came to the door. Slowly, he came to the quiet and murky realization that no one was home, or they were refusing to come to the door. He felt faint and suddenly pictured himself dying alone on that staircase. Clarity came to him briefly: *He had to return to where he would be found and helped.*

Matthew managed to run down the wooden staircase and back around the side of the building, towards Main Street. His awareness became utterly fragmented then. At some point, he realized he was down on the ground in the street, back by the Silver Dollar. Someone, likely Jason, gently helped him to the ground, applied pressure to his wounds, and covered him up.

Now he is aware that his phone is ringing. But he cannot, for the life of him, answer it. Jake arrives at his side, and Matthew asks Jake

42

to call his parents, Andrew and Kris Ortega. Once they pick up, Jake tells them that Matthew has been shot, that they should come right away. Going in and out of consciousness, Matthew is also aware of Laura, the bartender, shaking him gently and talking to him. Then the adrenaline that fueled his flight down the street, up and down a stairwell, and back to the site of the crime, fully dissipates. Matthew finally completely loses consciousness.

Just after he was shot, Gavin Faulkner dragged himself from vehicle to vehicle with bullet wounds in his thigh and hand. Between vehicles, he saw Davis continue to shoot his friends. He took momentary shelter behind a white truck and tried to get a better look at where Davis was. Through the light created by the gun blasts, he was finally able to calculate that there was enough steel between him and Davis that he could take off running. His goal was the residence behind the Claim Jumper, where his aunt and uncle lived. He knew that Brad went home earlier, letting his staff close up the bar. Gavin knew his aunt and uncle would be home and able to help him. As he ran, he became aware that his gait was uneven.

Now, as he stands on the porch of his aunt and uncle's home, under its bright light, he sees blood running down his legs. But still, he can't quite decipher what is happening to him. As he pounds on their door, he sees giant red splatters left by his fist. Now comes the pain and the realization that he was in fact hit by multiple bullets.

Gavin's uncle, Brad DiIorio, throws open the door. Gavin sees him standing there, the porch light glinting off his uncle's bald head. Brad's surprised, perplexed, and loving face finally allows Gavin to acknowledge how injured he is. His aunt, Kelly DiIorio, hastily ushers him inside. She binds up his leg and his hand, gently murmuring comforting words that Gavin cannot discern. Meanwhile, Brad races out to bring the truck around.

Brad transports his nephew down Main Street, the brief mile and a half to Madison Valley Hospital. Neither speaks. Brad has not yet pieced together that the man he instinctively deemed a menace and ejected from his own bar, is the same one who caused the mayhem he sees now on Main Street. On the way to the hospital, neither Gavin nor Brad can believe what is happening in their beloved town. The wailing panic siren; clustered confused groups of people, some of them screaming; and bodies everywhere. Right then, the ambulance pulls into the road, driving the same way as they are, lights flashing and siren bleating. How did their town turn into a war zone?

Only about 20 minutes earlier, Stan Klaumann, Jason's father, had heard his pager go off. He was already awake because of the ruckus outside. He'd heard the blasts through his open bedroom window. But he, like so many others, shrugged it off as fireworks. The bars were only blocks from his house, and he always expected some noisy nights once the college kids were back home. But then his pager went off. The dispatcher first said there was one victim. Stan catapulted himself out of bed, threw on clothes, and raced to the Ambulance Barn. He heard vehicles sliding to a stop in the parking lot outside, other team members arriving to help.

Around then, a second page came in, saying there were seven victims. *Seven? What on earth?* Then his son called. Jason named each of those seven victims. Every single name brought up a face, a family. Stan was grateful for this knowledge, and horrified.

He hung up with Jason, and another EMT flung open the side door and reported for the run. Stan greeted Susie Sprout, the Ennis Deputy Town Clerk. She was just given the Ennis Lion's Club "Citizen of the Year" award the night before. Stan brought her up to speed, "Dispatch just corrected the number of victims from one to seven." Susie's face turned pale. She said her son, Michael Sprout, had planned to go downtown for the evening. Susie was momentarily paralyzed by what this particular ambulance run could possibly mean for her, as a mother. Stan put his hand on her shoulder. Because of Jason's call, he was able to immediately comfort and convince her that Michael should be okay.

In very short order, the entire team of EMTs and First Responders of the Ennis Volunteer Ambulance reported for duty at the Ambulance Barn: Stan Klaumann, Brad and Barbara Bradshaw, Susie Sprout, Ginger and Andrew Guinn, Steve Loucks, Wade Miller, and Jamie Neiswander. They all rose from bed, dressed, and hurried out the door, as they had done on countless other occasions. They assigned duties, then screamed downtown, siren and lights blazing, and began the transports. These dutiful and courageous souls would stabilize and transport two of the most severely injured: Matthew Ortega and Mike Carroll. Their night would begin with caring for these two men. But it would not end there.

Nicole and Angie had done their best to pull Mike and Ginger inside, off the front steps of the Silver Dollar. Neither Mike nor Ginger was very responsive at that time. Nicole leaned down into Mike's face and quietly said, "Mike, what do you want us to do for you?" Both young women waited, holding their breath, ready to take orders.

"I don't know, I don't know," Mike answered, just as quietly.

They turned their attention and their caring faces to Ginger. They spoke to her, but she didn't answer them, which brought fresh terror to the girls. They murmured to each other, wondering what on earth they could or should do. Nicole only knew that she must hold Ginger tightly and try to keep her conscious.

Angie then took off, running. Rational or not, her body powered her out the door, thinking the police still had not been called. Many people did not own cell phones yet, and so she could think of only one thing: *She needed to find a phone, away from the chaos.* She flew down Main Street, quickly clearing the considerable distance to the Town Pump Gas Station. Her heart was pumping hard, and she was startled to hear the sound of her own screaming. Tears poured down her face as she ran. She screamed so much she was unaware of the panic alarm when it began its persistent wail into the moonlit night.

Doug Clark, who broke Mike's fall, catching him in his arms, is now with his own son, relentlessly continuing CPR. Jamie seems lifeless, but Doug cannot give up. Scott Wright, another Ennis High

School graduate, is suddenly at his side. Doug asks for help, and together they gently load Jamie's body into the back of Scott's pickup truck. Scott hands Doug his keys, and Doug speeds to Madison Valley Hospital where his wife, Sharon, is waiting for him.

Meanwhile, Scott stays on at the scene. He has a military background and realizes his training is needed here. Scott and Jason begin working in tandem, tending to the wounded, calming the panicked. Soon, as the police arrive, they also provide valuable information and assist with crowd control. Jason will later credit Scott for his calm and assertive demeanor, his constant sense of how to effectively stabilize each situation. In their own minds, neither of these men does anything exceptional. They simply act on their solid foundations of emergency response training. They'll each insist: *Anyone else with similar training would have done the same.*

Don Schaufler, who lived about a quarter mile past Main Street, woke to what he instinctively knew were gunshots. Not fireworks. Then he heard a car speeding past his house. With a sense of foreboding, he dressed and jumped into his Suburban. As he approached downtown, he heard people screaming: *He's shooting everybody! Where is he? He might come back!*

He saw people lying on the sidewalk and others still crouching for cover alongside parked cars. He saw a man laying a body into the back of his pickup. Don too, felt like he was entering a war zone. He continued driving through the horrific scene, looking for where he could be of assistance.

As Don parks his vehicle, he is drawn to the largest knot of people, outside the Silver Dollar. He pushes through the crowd to get into the bar, where the crowd clusters around a body. He realizes the body is Ginger Powers, whom he recognizes as a friend of his own daughters. He learns that Mike was also shot and was just transported by the ambulance. Don gently lifts Ginger, with the help of Nicole and others. Together they carry her to Don's vehicle, and he transports her to Madison Valley Hospital. Like so many others, he sees the need and fills it—with no clear knowledge of whether a life-threatening danger could still be present.

Having asked the gas station clerks to call the police, Angie begins her return run back to the Silver Dollar where she meets Nicole outside. She learns that Ginger and Mike have been transported to Madison Valley Hospital. The two girls hug each other tightly for a long moment. Then, deeply concerned about their wounded friends, the two walk the half mile to the hospital, arm in arm, in tight, tense silence, not at all sure what they will find when they get there.

DEPUTY SHERIFF DAVID CLARK, Ennis High School Class of 1989

Officer David Clark had felt slight misgivings when he went on duty that night: *A Friday the 13th. And a full moon.* All superstitions aside, talk to any law enforcement officer or emergency services provider, and they'll tell you, "Full moons bring out the crazies." He was sure the concurrence would have some effect on the next several hours. He was the only officer on duty that night in the Madison County Sheriff's Office over in Virginia City. A lonely shift.

Clark was in the Evidence Room, checking in new materials, when the dispatch call came in. The first words he heard were "multiple gunshot wounds." This alarmed him, but not nearly so much as when the dispatcher repeated, and clarified, the latest information. *Correction: multiple gunshot wound victims.*

Clark bolted out of the office to his patrol car, then headed over the Virginia City Pass towards Ennis at an estimated speed of 100 miles per hour. He noticed only two other vehicles coming in the opposite direction, as he tore through the night. He felt the weight of being totally alone at that moment. There was so much that he didn't know about the situation awaiting him. For the time being, he focused on the highly tactical mountain drive.

Certainly, what he didn't know far outweighed what he did. He didn't know how many victims there were; he didn't know if the victims were dead or alive; he didn't know how many perpetrators there were; he didn't know if the situation was "ongoing" or not; he didn't know who, or where, the perpetrator was.

When he rounded the bend into the straightaway that became Ennis's Main Street, he took in the dark mob of terrified citizens, and saw multiple clusters of need. His brain began to triage. For a moment, his ingrained training competed with his emotions—which he expediently suppressed. He had to.

He slid his vehicle into a space in front of the Silver Dollar, the stated epicenter of the tragedy. Upon entry, he found sheer and utter chaos. Vomit and blood covered the floor, and the panic alarm was still blaring. Two bodies were on the floor, and a frantic and noisy group of community members knotted around them. People were clearly trying to help, shoving and shouting advice. Some were inadvertently and unknowingly creating more chaos.

But some of the citizens were providing genuinely valuable help. Outside, he saw some bodies loaded into private vehicles, heading for the hospital. He heard the blare of the ambulance siren and was grateful professional help would arrive in seconds. Within another minute, one of the victims in the bar was being tended to by EMTs.

Clark knew most of the people all around him. He recognized most of the gunshot victims. He felt the atmosphere shift as he entered the bar and again as the EMTs arrived. The volume literally dropped. Everyone was grateful to see a man in uniform, so anxious to have someone in charge. Officer David Clark, age 31, husband to Dulcie, father of two young boys, shouldered that mantle.

Within minutes, Officer Clark starts interviewing all those who are both present and coherent. He immediately determines the most concerning fact: the shooter's whereabouts are currently unknown. Then he finds two familiar faces: Jason Klaumann and Scott Wright. He already knows the depth of character of both of these men. They are more than witnesses; they can be a genuine help to him. He asks them to assist him in identifying other key witnesses, and in the more general surveillance and calming of the chaotic scene.

Officer Tom Tighe, the Ennis Chief of Police, arrives from his home 20 miles away. The Madison County Sheriff, David Schenck, also arrives, as well as Deputies David Birdsill and Phillip Fortner. Soon, all six members of the Madison County Sheriff's Department are on the scene, some having traveled from the other side of sprawling Madison County.

Officers Clark and Fortner speak with Laura Clark, the bartender, and obtain the name of the suspect: *George Davis*. Now they have a name. Other witnesses in the bar tell them that Davis works as a ranch hand at the Bar 7, at the far south end of the valley.

Officer Clark advises Sheriff Schenck that he believes the Montana Department of Justice should be called in. The sheriff agrees, and they make the call. Now the State of Montana Law Enforcement Network, with its information-sharing protocol, slides into full gear. But no one yet knows that Davis is closing the gap, at break-neck speed, towards his next set of victims, nearly 200 miles away.

Officers Clark and Fortner get in their separate cars and speed the 30 miles to the Bar 7 Ranch. They bang on every door on every building and get no answer. As all appears dark, and they see no sign of Davis or his vehicle, they return to town. Along the way, Officer Clark gets a flat tire and must leave his vehicle at D&D Auto. He rides with Officer Fortner the rest of the way back. The two young officers are finally allowed a moment to breathe and give brief comfort to one another as colleagues, to reflect on what has transpired in these early morning hours.

# Chapter 5

## *Saving Lives*

Nurse Jaime Singleton Roberts has been on shift at Madison Valley Hospital since midnight on June 14. She and Nurse Jan Brooks have been quietly chatting on this still, summer night. The hospital has no patients, and both women have worked here for decades. At approximately 1:45 a.m., they hear successive loud reports, and they look at each other with raised brows. The same thought races through each woman's mind. *Fireworks? Or gunshots?*

Nurse Roberts is sure that it's fireworks, a rational assumption considering the Fourth of July is only a couple of weeks away. Nurse Brooks, however, does not agree, and the two head outside, standing under the covered front entrance of the hospital, which sits on a plateau less than a block away from Main Street. They can hardly believe what they hear: more of what they now know to be gunshots, followed by a woman screaming. They hear muffled panic, loud shouts, car doors slamming, confusion, and fear, and then they hear a panic alarm piercing the once peaceful night.

They hurriedly confer, and Nurse Brooks takes up the phone. Her first call is to alert and summon the physician's assistant on duty that night, Ben Lindeman. PA Lindeman has been on call for three days straight, as a *locum*, out of Community Hospital in Missoula. He is catching a little sleep in the Fan Mountain Inn directly across the two-lane highway from the hospital. He answers the 1:50 a.m. call, and Nurse Brooks tells him what they've heard. He tells her that he'll be there immediately. PA Lindeman dresses and literally sprints across the moonlit highway to join Nurse Roberts, who is waiting for him at the front entrance to the small hospital.

The Madison County Sheriff's Department Dispatch has now received Jason Klaumann's call. The dispatcher on duty officially notifies Nurse Brooks of the situation and the number of suspected injuries and casualties. Nurse Brooks, in turn, telephones the entire nursing and lab staff of Madison Valley Hospital. She awakens Nurses Jody Sprout and Linda Ryan, along with Lab Technician Tana Bowles (Overcast-Becher). None live in town, but all three are immediately on their way. They hastily dress and leave their sleeping families, barely believing that they have been summoned to attend "multiple gunshot victims." Nurse Roberts and PA Lindeman as yet have no concept of what they will encounter as they walk together toward the hospital's emergency entrance. The sounds coming from downtown are unlike anything they have ever heard, and they try to generate some semblance of calm between them as they see headlights approaching fast.

A car screams into the parking area bringing in a young man who has a gunshot wound in his thigh. They meet the first survivor at the emergency room doors: Trett Sutter, with his mother, Patricia. Nurse Roberts ushers them in, and one of the private hospital rooms is hastily prepared for Trett. Patty telephones her sister, Peggy Nestegard, who summons her employer, Margaret Bortko, a Nurse Practitioner in Ennis.

Just then, a pickup truck drives up. PA Lindeman and Nurse Roberts realize, to their near disbelief, that there is a body in the bed of the pickup. At that moment, they begin to grasp the breadth of what is truly happening. PA Lindeman quietly whispers to Nurse Roberts, "We are going to have a lot of work to do tonight." Sharon Clark, who arrived in her own vehicle, rushes over to the pickup. The driver of the truck tumbles out and wails, "Please, save my son!" Physician and nurse both jump into the pickup bed. The patient is Jamie L. Roberts. His father, Doug, tries to describe the horror he's witnessed downtown. The two medical providers glance at each other, realizing that tonight will take all that they can possibly summon, and that many lives are truly, and inexorably, in their hands. But as of now, they have no idea what challenges they will face in mere minutes.

The two elevate the torso of the young man in the back of the pickup truck, and PA Lindeman begins resuscitation and chest compressions, both counting together. The PA and nurse meet eyes over the head of Jamie Roberts. *They can't possibly help this boy.* Still, they carry out several rounds of CPR. PA Lindeman rests a gentle palm alongside Jamie's neck, and he quietly pronounces him dead. Nurse Roberts turns to Doug and Sharon Clark, about to tell them what they cannot accept: They have one son, and he is dead.

But right then, the ambulance pulls into the hospital emergency entrance, with lights flashing and siren blaring. Even more private vehicles are careening in too. Nurse Roberts briskly gestures to PA Lindeman that he should go, and he reluctantly climbs off the truck bed, then rushes to meet the ambulance. Nurse Roberts holds back. Doug begs her once more, "Please, Jaime, do something!" She knows this family and this boy. Out of irrational love, she returns to the boy's side. She leans over the quiet body of the young man whose name is identical to her own, Jamie Roberts, and she performs CPR yet again, alone. His young face is cooling. Still, she searches for signs of life, and again, finds none. She has to tell them. She takes a deep breath, faces his parents, and tells them the hard truth. Then she has to go. She has no choice; more victims are arriving. Reluctantly, she leaves the couple to mourn on their own.

She joins PA Lindeman, as Mike Carroll and Matthew Ortega are transferred out of the Ennis ambulance. Both the young men are gravely wounded and barely conscious, and both have been shot in the torso. They are brought inside the hospital, and PA Lindeman immediately instructs the staff on how to set up these critical patients in the two opposing beds of the emergency room. Nurse Roberts had only met PA Lindeman that night. As they work side by side, she sees that she is in league with a true professional. The PA exercises firm control of each new crisis.

More arrive. Nurse Roberts recognizes each young victim, her mind flooded with memories of each one as a unique person, little details about each of their families. PA Lindeman doesn't know any of these young people, yet their lives are in his hands. *Maybe that's a good thing.* He moves fast, immediately assessing and directing the now swarming hospital corridors, full of victims, nurses, EMTs, parents of the victims, and community members who have come to do anything they possibly can to help.

Brad DiIorio arrives with his nephew, Gavin Faulkner, and Nurse Roberts sees that the young man has been shot in the hand and the thigh. EMTs approach them, and Brad reluctantly releases his nephew into their care. Gavin is laid on a gurney and steered into one of the only four private rooms.

Don Schaufler drives up, and EMTs meet him and transfer a young woman out of his vehicle. Nurse Roberts recognizes Ginger Powers; she has known this girl her entire life. Ginger has been shot in the pelvis and thigh and is clearly in critical condition. A place is hastily readied for her on the x-ray table, across the hall from the two young men in the emergency room. Nurse Roberts and others make Ginger as comfortable as they possibly can. There are no formal beds left.

The small rural Madison Valley Hospital, a Critical Access Hospital, is now stretched to its capacity. The formal emergency room's two beds are full, the two private hospital rooms are full, and they've had to place one critically injured patient on the x-ray table for lack of another hospital bed. At least the steady stream of intakes seems to have finally abated.

Nurse Roberts is in the room with Ginger when EMT Susie Sprout comes in and hails her. "Isaiah is here," she says meaningfully. Susie knows that Isaiah Crowley has been living with Nurse Roberts and her husband, Shorty, for a year. She knows they love him like one of their own children. Running on autopilot, Nurse Roberts says briskly, "Please tell him to wait for me in the waiting room." She assumes that Isaiah has heard the commotion in town and is there to check on her. Susie looks at her and gently but firmly clarifies, "No, Jaime, Isaiah has been shot."

Nurse Roberts had not seen Shorty arrive with Isaiah in their family truck. This boy, who is like a son to her, has been shot in the hip, back, hand, and wrist. EMTs have stretchered him into the one remaining private hospital room. Nurse Roberts braces herself, as any mother would, for what she may deal with next.

Right at that moment, PA Lindeman passes by, grabbing her by the arm, to bring her with him to assess Isaiah. He has no idea that she is Isaiah's "Ennis mother." When they enter the room, Isaiah is conscious and alert. Upon seeing her face, he says, "I'm so very glad you're here!" There is a pause as everyone in the room takes in the gravity of Isaiah's wounds—and the fact that one of his medical providers is his mother. Nurse Roberts must now summon all her professional comportment, as her maternal feelings threaten to overwhelm the clear-headedness she needs to provide wise and timely care.

Isaiah seems aware of this. The young man senses his mother's control of his own medical emergency. His breathing steadies, and he settles into the fight for his life. He knows that he is supported by not only caring professionals, but by the family love of his Ennis parents. Together, PA Lindeman and Nurse Roberts lean over Isaiah's vulnerable body and examine the four bullet wounds, determining the best options to stabilize him.

Nurse Roberts has, at some point, assisted all the victims now. The others are being well tended by EMTs and other nursing staff. She allows herself to be present in this room only, to bear the mantle of "mother of a victim," and she settles into tending Isaiah, as both mother and experienced nurse.

Nurse Practitioner Margaret Bortko had been at home with her teenaged son and several of his friends who were spending the night. She woke to the call from Peggy, the office manager of her newly formed Community Health Center. Peggy's nephew, Trett Sutter, had been shot and was at the hospital. NP Bortko hastily dressed and sped to the hospital only blocks away from her home. She was prepared to see a few vehicles belonging to Peggy's family. What she saw was a very different scene.

She arrived as other vehicles were pulling in. The ambulance was already there, EMTs milled about, and a large crowd of people stood outside the emergency room entrance. It was a chaotic calm. There was no shoving, no mobbing at the door, but an obvious panic pervaded, laced with that somber sense of "waiting for news." As she moved through the quiet crowd outside the hospital, she felt them part respectfully, with the knowledge that a community member with medical training was here to help.

NP Bortko first encountered Doug and Sharon Clark frozen at the emergency entrance, mourning. In an instant, she realized that the still form in the back of the pickup was their son, Jamie. She rested a hand on Doug's shoulder, knowing it was paltry comfort. She also knew she had to get inside and try to make some sense of the scenes bombarding her.

Once in the hospital, NP Bortko saw all the young people, some conscious, some not. Because of her Advanced Trauma Life Support Training, she was immediately aware of the severe condition of the critically injured trio: Mike, Ginger, and Matthew. She silently prayed that medical transport was on the way. In hasty conversation with PA Lindeman, she assisted in triaging the situation: determining who needed what type of attention and in what order. Then she dove in, helping the nurses and the physician's assistant provide that care.

NP Bortko raised her family in Ennis. She was tied to each of the patients in the emergency room. She saw Ginger, the daughter of Marilyn Powers, a woman who has worked in the hospital with the cleaning staff. She saw Matt Ortega and Isaiah Crowley, young men whose families she knows. She knew Trett Sutter as the nephew of her office manager. She also recognized Gavin and Mike.

Matthew's condition was of grave concern. NP Bortko conferred with PA Lindeman about what may be a bullet wound to his spleen. They determined that his left lung was silent, collapsed. She wanted very much for this young man to not be alone, and she worried that he may not survive. She remembered that the Ortegas lost a son several years earlier in a drowning accident at Ennis Lake. Her heart was full of this, what his parents must be going through. She called Matthew's parents, Andy and Kris, out of the waiting room, bringing them to their son's side.

Nurse Jody Sprout, a decades-long respected member of the Madison Valley Hospital nursing staff, was at home asleep when Nurse Brooks called about a gunshot wound victim. Nurse Sprout leapt out of bed, dressed, and drove from her home, about 15 minutes south of Ennis. To get to the hospital, she had to drive through the crime scene downtown. She saw the flashing lights, crime scene tape being unfurled, multiple police vehicles, crowds of panicked people. She'd thought she was heading to care for an errant gun injury to a single person. She quickly realized that this was something far worse.

Nurse Sprout parked her vehicle in the crowded parking lot, and then she too felt that respectful parting of the crowd, allowing her entry into the hospital. Tana Bowles (Overcast- Becher), a longtime lab technician at Madison Valley Hospital, met Nurse Sprout at the door and told her where to find PA Lindeman. Tana also let her know that she was standing by in the hospital lab to provide blood-typing as needed.

Once Nurse Sprout found PA Lindeman, he instructed her to set up a mobile x-ray cart to provide x-rays of all the young victims. She hastily did so and began to travel between the rooms. Her first patient was Ginger Powers. The young woman was lying on her back on the x-ray table, with Nurse Roberts and an EMT attending to her. Nurse Sprout asked for their assistance in turning Ginger onto her side, to obtain the needed image.

The three women saw and heard the metallic clatter of a bullet as it fell from Ginger's body. It rolled onto the hard surface of the x-ray table. There was a pause. For a moment, none of them could move, seeing the physical evidence of this heinous crime perpetrated against a young woman and mother. There was a collective breath, and then they all set back into action. Nurse Sprout took the x-ray, and the three staff gently turned Ginger onto her back again. All three were hit hard with an awareness of the gravity of the situation, and the suffering of their young patients.

Nurse Linda Ryan also received a call from Nurse Brooks, and likewise leapt into action, driving from her home ten minutes north of Ennis. She too, pushed through the ER doors and sought out PA Lindeman for instruction. Under his direction, Nurse Ryan began a rotation of all the patients, taking vitals and checking for signs of shock.

Right now, the shock in every room is thick, and not just among the patients. This early morning is unlike anything Nurse Ryan has yet experienced in her career. She immediately feels the overwhelming sadness emanating from all the medical personnel, EMTs, and parents in all the halls and rooms. Her senses are overloaded with this sadness and with this truth: *these people are trying to save the lives of their children or their children's good friends.* They have watched these young people grow up, given them vaccines, treated them for colds and flu infections, watched them make their way through elementary school, middle school, and high school. They've watched them play sports, go on first dates, and finally, become young adults. All the nurses and EMTs know their patients' parents, perhaps go to the same church with them, certainly see them in the grocery store. They live their lives together. It is this sadness with which Nurse Ryan is so profoundly overwhelmed as she enters each room.

Then, as she passes by the nurses' station, Nurse Ryan sees Doug Clark looking lost. His hands are covered in blood. They make eye contact.

"Where can I wash my hands?" he asks her. Then he tells her that he tried to save his son's life. It's his son's blood.

*Oh, this poor man!* Nurse Ryan gently guides him to a private bathroom where he can have a few moments. She cannot do anything more for him. She takes a deep breath and surges back into action, with her heart full of loving concern for all of them.

Martha Klaumann, the wife of Stan and mother of Jason Klaumann, also arrives at the hospital within minutes of the call from her son. Martha normally manages the hospital switchboard during daytime business hours. She immediately takes up that task. She also takes on the job of formally registering the patients.

She sets up her forms and clipboard and begins the needed but painful job of meeting with each patient's family to obtain necessary medical information. She connects first with Pat Carroll, mother of Mike Carroll, speaking with her gently and walking her through the weirdly mundane health history questions. Martha moves on to the next form, for Ginger Powers. The family is in the x-ray room with Ginger, who is still resting on the x-ray table. Martha realizes that, had her parents not been with her, she wouldn't have known Ginger. The usually vibrant young woman was unrecognizable. Martha gets through that form, then heads back to the switchboard. All the lines are lighting up. She's got to cover the phone for a while.

Then the emergency room doors swing open again, and Martha greets Nurse Joan Goetze. She was the last nurse summoned, once someone realized she was still in town and not on vacation as originally believed. Martha sends Joan off to PA Lindeman to receive an assignment. At this point, as Martha looks around, she realizes that every single member of the Madison Valley medical community is present in the hospital now. Everyone is here, providing the best medical care possible to save these beloved kids.

Matthew Ortega briefly woke while the EMTs stretchered him into the hospital. He came to with the shocking awareness that he was naked. He momentarily wondered whether people would notice and be offended. Then he promptly passed out again. At some point he became quite aware that he was drifting in and out of consciousness. He heard many sounds he couldn't identify. He heard loud shouting, directions and firm orders. Also, quiet utterances, voices asking how they can best help. It all happened in a dizzying cacophony around him.

Matthew is awake again right now. PA Lindeman enters the room and speaks directly to Matthew about what needs to be done to help him. The PA gently informs Matthew that he must insert a chest tube into his body, to inflate his collapsed left lung and save his life. He is frank with him then, "I cannot give you anything to numb the pain. This is going to be extremely uncomfortable." Fully alert now, Matthew consents to this, without any anesthetic, and with total confidence in the PA.

When PA Lindeman makes the incision into Matthew's side, the pain is searing. He sinks so low, loses a hold on his own life force, and he considers the possibility that he truly cannot bear this. He closes his eyes and feels at peace, gives himself over to the thought that maybe he is about to die. Maybe that wouldn't be so bad. His strong spiritual beliefs enable him to disappear into the peace and comfort of this other place away from the pain. But he doesn't die.

Matthew is suddenly entirely aware of his father, Andy Ortega, shaking him and desperately pleading with him to hold on. His parents' faces are close to his, both looking so familiar, yet tragic with their love and fear. He is seized with a clear understanding that he must survive this for the sake of his close-knit family—they are all still reeling from the loss of his brother, Justin.

His mother, Kris Ortega, holds tightly to his hand, and he knows it would cost her dearly to lose another son. Matthew knows then that he is not going to die. He knows that he will use every ounce of his strong character and human force to survive. He speaks to his parents then, promises them that he will live. Then he allows himself to fall back into the peaceful darkness.

Meanwhile, for PA Lindeman, the next moments, stretching into critical minutes and then hours, are filled with coordinating the care of each of the six wounded. Early in his career, the PA initially worked in pediatrics and general medicine, but he soon transitioned to his true love, emergency medicine. Even when he was in school, his Master of Sciences degree from A.T. Still University had an emphasis on emergency medicine. That past training and personal passion is now a blessing to the Ennis community.

PA Lindeman organizes and coordinates the lab testing, the x-rays, the Foley placements, and the IV placements, and he efficiently determines whether each patient needs blood. He communicates briskly with and directs his nurses, Jan Brooks, Jaime Singleton Roberts, Jody Sprout, Joan Goetze, and Linda Ryan, along with the laboratory technician, Tana Bowles (Overcast-Becher). He also gently but firmly manages the crowd within the small rural hospital's halls and rooms. In a smoothly orchestrated dance, all the medical professionals and volunteers on site are perfectly attuned to where they may lend a helping hand. Always at the forefront and maintaining order and direction, is PA Lindeman.

The instant that the PA determines each of his six patients is in stable condition, and that his nursing staff and EMTs are maintaining that stability, his next task is to get them all transported to medical facilities that have far more extensive medical, surgical, and rehabilitative services. He heads out of the patient rooms and gets on the phone.

He must buck the existing system and current procedures and protocols to obtain immediate placement for each patient. Normally, a great deal of "workup" must be completed before a larger medical facility will approve a patient transfer. This situation is not normal. Still, the PA must convince the person at the other end of the telephone line that, under these so exigent circumstances, such lengthy workups are not only unworkable for this small hospital, but also could lead to the death of one or more of the patients. One by one, he speaks with hospitals in Montana, Idaho, and Washington. One by one, he pleads his case, and despite preliminary resistance, his entreaties are eventually accepted. Two hospitals in Montana and one in Idaho are each open to immediately accepting one or two of the emergency transfers. PA Lindeman allows himself a moment of quiet gratitude to overtake him. Just one moment.

Then he begins coordinating the flights and vehicular transports. Because this community—and the whole state—have never experienced anything quite like this and have no protocol for the situation, the PA himself must determine where to land the helicopters, how to fuel them, and how to close the highway, all while considering "the preservation of evidence" should he, in fact, have any under his management on this night. He has the presence of mind to telephone Ennis Airport and obtain fuel deliveries for the transport helicopters. Typically, transport helicopters can only fly one way without refueling. This is a complication for most medical transports, and he solves the problem before it arises.

The helicopter landing area has not been "secured," which normally involves a legally required sheriff's presence. Again, this situation is far from normal. PA Lindeman pushes through the red tape to allow the helicopter landings without the usual law enforcement presence. The local and regional police officers and sheriff's deputies are all unavailable! The Madison County officers, who would normally provide this service, are all downtown assessing whether the community is still in danger from the perpetrator.

Right then, like an answer to a prayer not yet uttered, the Ruby Valley EMTs arrive on scene in full force and quickly assess this immediate need. The Ruby Valley team is familiar with helipad preparation for the Sheridan Hospital, and they get to work on that task, ensuring that their Madison County colleagues can remain in the patient rooms. They apply their expertise, setting up the necessary emergency helipad on Highway 287, just in front of the hospital.

Freed momentarily from his phone work, PA Lindeman returns to the patient rooms. He assesses and reassesses all six patients, three of whom are critically wounded. He also continues to prevent well-meaning but non-medically credentialed people from causing inadvertent harm. He does not know the community well, and so he relies constantly on his nurses to let him know which people are actual family members, briskly determining who should and should not be inside the hospital. As often as he can, he speaks directly with those family members, trying to sound reassuring toward them, all the while privately wondering where the shooter or shooters could now be. *Could this night still get worse?*

Between patient checks and family conversations, he continues to field calls from the hospitals in Billings, Bozeman, and Idaho Falls, which have agreed to receive all the patients. *Which patient is going where and why? What surgical care will each one require?* In the midst of all that, the on-call physician arrives late in the action, having had surgery on her arm the day before. He tries to be diplomatic with her, doing his best to provide a complete summary of the six-patient emergency, though the situation is changing by the second. The PA conferences with all his staff and NP Bortko, and finally determines the order of transport: Matthew Ortega will be the first transport; he will be air-flighted to Eastern Idaho Regional Medical Center in Idaho Falls. Ginger Powers and Isaiah Crowley will be flown to St. Vincent's Healthcare in Billings, Montana. Finally, Mike Carroll, Gavin Faulkner, and Trett Sutter will be transported by ambulance to Bozeman Deaconess Hospital.

As patients, family, and medical staff facilitate the transports, a welcome helper shows up. Chaplain Warren Hiebert arrives from Bozeman, ready to offer heartfelt and professional assistance. Chaplain Hiebert is a 30-year veteran of the Gallatin County

Sheriff's Department. He spends time with the crowd outside the hospital entrance and with the victims' families. He quickly steps in to serve as a liaison between the medical staff and the parents and the crowd outside. His calm and loving presence offers solace and spiritual guidance to any who reach out for it.

The first helicopter arrives. The medical transport team gently awakens Matthew and transfers him to their stretcher. As Matthew gains a sense of his surroundings, he sees that he is leaving the hospital. He sees the lifeless form of Jamie Roberts, lying in the back of a pickup truck, and he is overwhelmed with sadness. Then Matthew remembers his decision to survive. He feels a flood of determination well up within him. A deep strength and faith take over as he is loaded into the helicopter.

All five of the other patients are transported out that night as well. Ginger Powers (Nelson) is air-flighted to St. Vincent's Healthcare in Billings, which will care for the bullet wounds to her abdomen and left thigh. Her mother, Marilyn Powers, takes the helicopter flight with her.

Isaiah Crowley, who was hit by four bullets in his back, hip, wrist, and hand, is also air-flighted to St. Vincent's Healthcare in Billings, where he will undergo surgery for all four wounds. Nurse Roberts (his mother) never leaves Isaiah's side until he is transported.

Finally, the regional ambulance transports begin. Mike Carroll, who has suffered a bullet wound to his pancreas, is transported by the first ambulance to Bozeman Deaconess Hospital. His mother, Patricia Carroll, rides with him.

Gavin Faulkner is treated in Madison Valley Hospital for the bullet wounds to his thigh and hand, then sent by ambulance to Bozeman Deaconess Hospital. His family meets him there.

Trett Sutter is in Madison Valley Hospital the longest of any of the victims. His bullet wound to the muscle in his thigh is deemed "fortunate," as it did not hit bone. He assures all present that, even though he is the first to arrive and the last to leave, that is all right with him. He generously understands that all the others have more serious injuries. Finally, an ambulance is freed up and arrives to take him to Bozeman Deaconess as well.

By mid-morning, all six of the shooting survivors have arrived at the hospitals that will provide needed surgeries and continued care. They all survive.

Nurses Jody Sprout, Jaime Roberts, Jan Brooks, Linda Ryan, Joan Goetze, Lab Technician Tana Bowles (Overcast-Becher), NP Bortko, and all the EMTs have been in the Madison Valley Hospital till well after sunrise. As the final transport departs, the hospital transitions from chaos to a still emptiness. Then another team of angels arrives from over 60 miles away. The Gallatin County EMTs show up to relieve the Ennis EMTs, so they can get some much-needed sleep. Every single Ennis crew member has been serving here all night.

They are taxed. They all desperately need sleep, but that leaves no one to cover the ambulance on a busy weekend day. No one to cover the normal emergencies in this region—heart attacks, boating accidents, falls. The Gallatin County EMTs will stand watch for them for several hours.

All the medical personnel finally have the opportunity to mutually share, mingle, and reflect with each other, processing all their medical lifesaving efforts. They feel a deep abiding satisfaction, laced with total exhaustion, for having done their absolute best. Nurse Ryan reflects on the strength of all the young patients—all graduates of Ennis High School, all children to her, but young adults now. She is struck by their bravery in the midst of such stress and pain. Even though all the patients are young, they all exhibited such quiet fortitude and strength.

A weary Nurse Sprout works with Lab Technician Bowles (Overcast-Becher) and EMT Barbara Bradshaw to strip all the beds and mop the blood off the floors. They bundle dirty linens and remake hospital beds. When they finish their work, they shake their heads in amazement and wonder to see that there are virtually no signs remaining of what transpired in those early morning hours.

They are all proud of PA Lindeman's efforts, his cool-headed leadership, and his medical expertise. That leadership provided them with the steadying influence the situation demanded. They are honored to have worked under his direction, and they feel they were anchored by his calm countenance, compassion, rational decision-making, medical judgment, and doggedness with the tertiary care center directors. His judgment calls directly contributed to the excellent outcomes for all the living patients.

71

Due to PA Lindeman's herculean efforts in promoting, persuading, cajoling, and demanding help from hospitals in Montana and Idaho, the patient-transfer procedures and protocols in those two states will be permanently altered and streamlined. He has successfully stretched the awareness of the tertiary care facilities, making it clear that, in certain situations, small community hospitals and their patients can be gravely harmed by stringent rules and regulations.

Simultaneously, as the medical team debriefs and celebrates all that went well that morning, they also think of Jamie Roberts. They grieve for him and for his daughter, his wife, his sister, and his parents. They grieve also for the brokenness that their whole town will feel, as everyone else soon hears the news.

NP Margaret Bortko returns home to her still-sleeping teenage son and his friends. She wakens them and provides them with a highly abbreviated summary. She can't tell them much, but she has to tell them something, as she wants to take them all back to their homes. At this point, no one knows where the shooter is. She decides it would be best for each of the kids to be with their respective families, and she drives around town taking each boy home.

Finally, Margaret heads home. On the way, she stops at the Town Pump to buy a pack of cigarettes. She hasn't smoked in years. But this morning, she sits outside on her deck overlooking Ennis. She lights a cigarette and reflects on the last several hours, on all the life-saving decisions. She is overwhelmed with peace that every action taken was the right one. She doesn't know how each of the patients will fare, but she is proud to have been part of a team that gave each patient the best possible chance for survival.

Margaret waits for it to get late enough to call a relative who also works in the critical care world. She badly needs to decompress, to talk with someone who will understand what she is feeling. The cigarettes are not enough. She looks down at the town and the sun glinting off the Madison River. She quietly reflects on the innumerable ripple effects that will likely emanate from this night's ordeal, how it will test this small town, spread out before her in the glittering sunlight.

# Chapter 6

## *Morning*

Early Saturday morning, like any other summer day, the sun still streamed in everyone's windows. High over the rooftops, a gentle cool breeze sifted through the ancient cottonwoods. Those trees would offer a respite of cool shade as the day heated up. With the summer solstice only a week away, the sun rose before most people did. But as the town awoke, the lines of communication began to hum. Anyone who didn't know what happened overnight, soon learned. This was no normal Saturday. Life in Ennis would not feel normal for a long time.

The EMS workers and hospital staff had to keep the details of the night to themselves, respecting their patients and the integrity of the investigation. However, local young people who had been downtown and witnessed the horror communicated with those who hadn't been there—the news spread fast. The stream of information emanating from the people involved tangentially began to roll out a concerned and shimmering web from citizen to citizen.

As the town awoke, Sheriff David Schenk maintained tight control over all of Main Street, while a team of his own officers and others from agencies all over the region gathered evidence. That team, assembled within hours after the shooting, worked meticulously behind the yellow crime scene tape, which cordoned off a two-block stretch of Main Street. Typically, this part of town would soon fill with vehicles on such a brilliant sunny Father's Day weekend. This was after all, a fishing town, and Father's Day was the summertime equivalent of Black Friday for many of the businesses, second only to the Fourth of July.

For now, the heart of Ennis was blocked by yellow tape and police car barricades. Traffic was detoured through the residential street directly south of Main. Shops were not closed, but locals and tourists alike had to park at the far ends of town and walk along Main Street to get to the heart of the historic business district.

Sheriff Schenk had held the office of Madison County Sheriff for only six months, but he was already well known, having raised his three children in Ennis while serving as a Montana Highway Patrol Officer. He had a warm and welcoming persona and was popular with the townspeople. His broad smile and crinkly eyes gave comfort to everyone he encountered before they even engaged in conversation.

That painful Saturday morning, he had been on site since minutes after the shooting. Like all the officers involved, by 9:00 a.m. he was starting to feel the weight of his fatigue, his position, and his own raw emotions regarding what had just transpired. Still, he plodded on, managing the evidence-gathering effort, and connecting with each worried business owner, every overly curious tourist, and the handful of locals who hadn't yet heard what happened last night. One by one, he had the same awkward conversation with several business owners:

"Excuse me, Sheriff, do you know when Main Street will open again?"

"We'll get this street open as soon as humanly possible. Our entire team is working toward that end. But we will likely need more than one day. I'm so sorry I can't give you a specific time."

"Have they caught him yet?"

"I've been assured that we are no longer under any immediate threat. I'll let you know the details as soon as I'm permitted to share them."

Then each shop owner would ask, "Should we close for the day? Or stay open?" Asking that question, their eyes all held the same sheepish look.

Sheriff Schenk couldn't make that choice for them, couldn't weigh the apples-to-oranges ethical comparison: *Close to honor the dead and wounded? Stay open as an act of defiance against the perpetrator?* He acknowledged the reality of that conundrum for every business owner and assured each one of them, "I understand and respect whatever you decide." He meant that. Then he reiterated, "We'll get this tape down and traffic moving normally, as soon as we possibly can."

Every conversation ended with the business owner downplaying their own concerns, "Oh Sheriff, you do your job and don't worry about us."

Ultimately, most businesses chose to stay open. But the detour and the crime scene tape had already caused much of the usual tourist traffic to continue on. Most of the cars headed north, people likely opting to start their Father's Day weekend with brunch in Harrison or Bozeman instead. None of the shopkeepers missed this fact. But none complained to Sheriff Schenk either. With him, they focused on their concerns for the families directly affected by the shooting and everyone's general safety.

Karen Swedman (Willett) and Eric Swedman kept the Madison Theatre open. They did so intentionally, hoping to provide a meeting place for the town's young people, somewhere they could go for quiet conversations, hugs, and healing. Other businesses made similar choices, staying open to support the locals. What they lost in tourist traffic that day, they gained in gratitude, fostering a sense of care and safety for all their bewildered and grieving friends.

Sheriff Schenk saw Glen Gallentine standing on the sidewalk outside his business, a fly-fishing shop two doors down from the Silver Dollar Saloon. Glen greeted the sheriff and asked all the usual questions, which could be answered with only the vaguest replies.

"Well, one thing I do know," Glen said, "none of this will change the true essence of our town."

"I couldn't agree more," the sheriff replied.

Sheriff Schenk wasn't yet allowed to share private information about the welfare of any of the survivors. Or Jamie. But as he walked, he saw and overheard shop owners huddled with each other, discussing whether to stay open and sharing what they did know about each of the survivors. These were details they'd gleaned through their collective grapevine of friends and family. *Who was still at the hospital here or in Bozeman? Who had been life-flighted to Billings or out of state? Who needed surgery?* This grapevine wasn't a bad thing. People cared; they wanted to know if everyone was okay. Or not. Everyone was reeling from this tragedy, this horror that had invaded this tightly knit business community and the individual lives of dear friends and family members.

As the morning progressed, a handful of stalwart tourists did stop and park at each end of town and loyally headed to favorite cafes and shops on foot. They approached the sheriff with curiosity, and he quickly honed a public line for the out-of-towners—a brisk narrative that at least assured them that no immediate danger existed anymore. "Some trouble last night, folks," he repeated over and over. "Nothing to worry about this morning."

Between his careful conversations with both locals and tourists, Sheriff Schenk made his way up and down both sides of the street, connecting with each of his own Madison County officers and those who had come to assist from Gallatin County. They all worked with careful focus, using tape to pull fingerprints off vehicles, hand brooms to gather shards of evidence from the ground, and cameras to photograph anything that could not be physically preserved. This was quickly becoming one of the biggest criminal cases Sheriff Schenk would handle in his career. With every new piece of evidence gathered, preserved, photographed, and recorded—casings, fingerprints, blood, signs of a scuffle—Sheriff Schenk felt deep gratitude to Gallatin County Sheriff Jim Cashell. He was the one who called in all this multi-department support in the early predawn hours. There was no way the local police force—comprising precisely one Ennis police officer and the County Sheriff's Department based in Virginia City—could have done this on their own.

# Chapter 7

## *The Chase*

Sheriff Schenk could not yet tell the citizens of Ennis why he was so sure that they were no longer under any immediate threat. But those details would soon be released to the press, and it would be all over the evening news. After wreaking havoc on the young people of Ennis, George Davis tore out of town on a county road heading west. Yes, that was the perpetrator's car that Don Schaufler heard speeding past his house, and yes, that was likely Davis screaming past Officer David Clark as his patrol car raced in the opposite direction, toward town. Davis hurtled through the dark, early morning hours, tearing westward along rural mountain highways. When he hit the Bitterroot Valley, he headed north toward Missoula.

A couple of hours after sunrise, a Ravalli County deputy pulled Davis over for speeding through the small town of Florence, Montana. The deputy had no idea he'd just stopped a suspect in a mass shooting; if he'd known, he would've called for reinforcements before even making the stop.

Instead, more mayhem ensued. Davis did pull over and stop, but he got out of his car shooting at the officer. Bystanders at a near-by convenience store ran for cover and called 911. The deputy was wearing body armor, but one bullet managed to hit his shoulder. He was able to return fire and get to safety. Then Davis got back in his car and tore back out onto the highway.

All surrounding counties were notified at this point. Davis was now on a major highway and couldn't hide. Highway Patrolman Jason Hildenstab and Missoula County Sheriff's Deputy David Conway heard the call, saw Davis's Taurus, and each gave chase.

Davis headed west on Highway 12 into the harrowing Lolo Pass—over a hundred miles of tightly winding mountain road heading for the Idaho border. Within ten miles of the state line, Davis jammed on his brakes, forcing Hildenstab's patrol car to crash into him. Both vehicles stopped, and once again, Davis got out of his vehicle shooting.

The officers returned fire, but Davis got back in his car and sped off yet again. With Hildenstab's car now undriveable, both officers got in Conway's vehicle and resumed the chase. Finally, an Idaho state trooper at the top of the mountain pass heard the calls for reinforcements. He was able to lay a spike strip across the road just before Davis's car appeared. The tires on the Taurus flattened. Still, Davis kept driving—and shooting—till he skidded sideways across the lane. Only after the patrol car broadsided him did Davis stop. He was, unimaginably, still alive. Davis was taken then, conscious and under constant police guard, to a hospital in Missoula with one bullet wound and several crash-related injuries.

This—the police chase after the rampage—would be the highlight of local and national television newscasts for weeks. Squad car cameras captured the shootouts, and that made for impressive evening news.

The shootout videos eventually disappeared from the news cycle, but the pain and work of recovery had only just begun. A community was in shock, its residents left to pick up the pieces of their broken town. That task fell to hundreds of diligent souls caring for each other for days and years to come.

# Chapter 8

## *Staying Open*

Gina Lopez was the best friend of Pat Carroll, Mike Carroll's mother. Despite a mostly sleepless night, Gina went to work at Madison Foods early Saturday morning. She and her husband had stood at Pat's side all night, at Bozeman Deaconess Hospital, until Mike was transported yet again, this time to Harborview Medical Center in Seattle, Washington. Years ago, the Lopezes had moved along with Pat and her family from central California to Ennis. Gina had known Mike since he was a baby.

Chris Gentry, the owner of the market, connected with each of her employees—all of them also her friends—and gently helped them carry on with their work on this incredibly emotional day. She took extra time with Gina, who had been through so much that night. They checked in with each other, sharing information.

Ken Sciuchetti, another employee and beloved member of the community, also circulated among fellow employees and customers, speaking gently with everyone he met. A husband, father, grandfather, and bus driver, he was a trusted soul who knew how to care for people in distress. Soon Chris, Gina, and Ken connected as a trio. It was clear to them that the grocery store had organically become a community meeting place that morning. Sure, local customers still came in for a few necessary weekend groceries, but they were also clearly here to find and connect with each other.

Chris and her two employees remarked how slowly all the customers made their way down each aisle. "There's a lot of hugs and tears," Gina said. "And groups of people sharing information."

Chris and Ken noticed another shift in their customers that morning. Usually when couples ran errands in this community, the wife would run in for a small grocery trip while the husband waited in their truck. "But this morning, the husbands aren't waiting in the parking lot; they're coming in too," Chris said. "The couples are shopping together, and they're both connecting with the friends they see in here."

Chris wanted to actively encourage this. "Let's make sure everyone knows the store is a safe place to meet," she said. She asked Gina to help get word out among the staff and customers. If everyone let one or two friends know, the whole town would know within a day. Gina was happy to help and left her boss and coworker to get started.

Chris confided in a hushed tone to Ken, "My daughter was invited downtown last night and almost went!" *How many other parents had that same feeling this morning?* "I am counting my blessings that I am not living every parent's worst nightmare right now." *But what about everyone who was?* The least Chris could do was foster a space where people could safely gather and care for each other. Ken put an assuring fatherly arm around his young boss, saying nothing, which was just the right thing to say.

All day long, Chris observed her customers and felt their helplessness and sadness. It was such a glorious June day outside, yet everyone carried a dark storm of grief in their hearts. Soon customers began to purchase an unusual number of party platters, sandwiches, meats and cheese, fruit, and baked goods. It became clear that people were gathering to share and connect in each other's homes or in community meeting places. Madison Foods had indeed become a gathering place, an outfitter of sorts, fostering the deeper connection that could only happen in people's homes and churches. Chris had purchased the store just that year, and she felt blessed to care for and give back to the close-knit community that was now her home.

While many small gatherings materialized all around Ennis that day, there was one that didn't happen: the bachelor party for Jason Klaumann's friend. The groom was a young fishing guide in town, another fellow Ennis High School graduate. He was friends with all of the survivors and especially with Jamie. What was supposed to be the second-most-joyful day in this young man's summer was now a day of utter shock and grief. He got the word out quickly and efficiently by telephone and tackle shops—since all the fishing guides met at the tackle shops before dawn on weekend days. Within hours, every angler in town knew of the tragedy and shared in the young man's shock.

When the Trading Post opened Saturday morning, the owners, Susan Muchmore and her son and daughter-in-law, Shad and

Cammie Sterzick, bunched closely around the cash register. Like everyone in Ennis, they shared grief and shock and information. As they spoke, a tourist came in. As the petite, gray-haired woman browsed the store, she couldn't help but overhear some of the conversation up at the cash register. Suddenly, the woman turned on her heels, headed out to her car, then returned to the shop holding a hand-painted flowerpot. She approached Susan and handed the adorable pot to her.

"I'm sorry for listening to your conversation," the woman said. "But, back home, when something bad happens to one of our own, we step right up and have an auction! I am so sorry to hear about your wounded young people, and I hope that this little flowerpot can be sold to someone who would like to help."

This woman with her donated flowerpot planted a seed in Susan's mind: an auction to benefit Jamie's family and the survivors of the shooting. It would only take a few weeks to pull it all together, and it all originated with the heartfelt sympathy of a total stranger.

# Chapter 9

## *Father's Day*

Officer David Clark's shift was scheduled to run from midnight to 8:00 a.m. That Saturday, it was about noon before he finally headed home to his wife, Dulcie, and their two young boys. Like any loving husband at the end of any workday, he hugged his wife. But that hug lasted a lot longer than usual—so long that their two small boys joined in. Eventually the boys grew restless and wandered away to play. David and Dulcie quietly conversed, doing their best to comfort each other, without letting on to the boys that their parents' world had been utterly shattered.

They couldn't talk for too long. David had to rest; his next shift would begin again late Saturday night. He knew he wouldn't sleep, but he lay down in bed anyway. He could not let go of the scenes he had witnessed—Jamie and each of the survivors, all young people he'd known their entire lives. He knew all the families, all their kids. He lay there, looking at the ceiling, until it was time to get up and put his uniform on again.

During his next overnight shift, in the predawn hours Sunday morning, Officer Clark got a call to investigate a burglar alarm that went off "up country" towards the south end of the valley. Still exhausted, but ready to focus on anything else, he climbed into his patrol car and sped south—the second time in 24 hours that he had to speed towards danger.

Dispatch canceled the call midway to his destination. False alarm. He pulled his car to the side of the road. Officer Clark took a moment to rest his head on his arms. He realized that he had been driving in a near black-out state of consciousness, with no awareness of his surroundings or what he was seeing along the way. About to pull back onto the highway and return to town, he consciously slammed on both his literal and mental brakes.

He needed to stay right here for a moment, parked on the shoulder. Adrenaline-fueled exhaustion, along with a deep concern for the victim and survivors, was threatening to overtake him. He said a prayer for the young survivors, now in hospitals in three different states, and for Jamie's family. He breathed for a minute or two. Then he gave himself a vigorous shake and headed back north through Ennis and on to Virginia City and his duty.

# Chapter 10

## *Prayer*

The prayer vigils began all over the valley as soon as everyone heard the news. Don Schaufler, who transported Ginger Powers to Madison Valley Hospital, and his wife, Trish, held a special prayer vigil in their own home right away on Saturday morning. They welcomed the members of their own church, the Ennis Assembly of God, and any other worshipers who wished to join in with them.

Sunday morning, every church in town—nine congregations total—had especially packed services. The prayers emanating from those services clearly served as a powerful gathering and galvanizing force for all the citizens of Ennis. Surely a love that powerful also reached and fortified each of the survivors in their far-flung hospital rooms.

# Chapter 11

## *Shaken But United*

**Ennis residents shaken, but united after shooting**

Kellyn Brown

*First printed in the Bozeman Daily Chronicle; June 28, 2003*

Ennis—a day after seven people were shot and one man was killed outside a bar here—residents are still shaken, but continue to show a resilience and pride one local said outsiders can't understand.

"What you're not seeing is the network in the community," said business owner Dan McClain. "It is rock solid right now."

McClain owns the Blue Heron gift shop on Main Street, which is about a block from the scene of the shooting.

"This is a real test for this community," he said. "And we're passing with flying colors."

Police tape still surrounded more than a block of Main Street Sunday, as investigators continued to comb the area for evidence, which may explain how and why a local ranch hand opened fire on a group of young people outside the Silver Dollar Saloon early Saturday morning.

The suspect then shot and wounded Ravalli county deputy sheriff Bernie Allestad, who tried to pull him over about six hours later.

George Harold Davis, 45, was shot in the abdomen following a police chase, which ended when two officers crashed their vehicles into his car near the Idaho border. He remains in intensive care in Missoula.

Davis allegedly killed 26-year-old Jamie Roberts of Ennis, a construction worker who was a four-year member of the Madison Valley Fire Department. The six other victims: Ginger Powers, 23; Mike Carroll, 24; Gavin Faulkner, 19; Isaiah Crowley, 24; Trett Sutter, 21; and Matthew Ortega, 22, all remain hospitalized.

Madison County Sheriff David Schenk said he did not know the conditions of the victims, but said most of them are still in intensive care.

Sunday, Schenk walked up and down Main Street telling business owners when the police tape would come down and directing tourists around the scene.

"The people in this town have been very supportive," Schenk said. "It's unfortunate we have to close the street for most of the day."

Business owners in the area seemed to understand.

"In the big picture, it is a minor inconvenience," said local realtor Dave Clark.

Clark stood with McClain in front of the Blue Heron. Like McClain, he was eager to point out the resilience of Ennis, describing the town of 840 people as "tough."

"We have to move on," Clark said. "This is kind of like a scar you take with you."

Madison Valley Real Estate, where Clark works, is across the street from the crime scene. Despite this, Clark said, "This is still a damn great place to live."

Glen Gallentine manages a fly shop two doors down from the Silver Dollar Saloon. He said the tragedy slowed what was expected to be a busy Father's Day weekend, but added "it will come back pretty quick."

"This is probably the friendliest little town in all the West," Gallentine said. "The type of place that shuts down when there's a ball game at the local school."

On the other side of town, about 75 people gathered at the Ennis Assembly of God Church.

Mark Elser, sitting in for Rev. George Ady, opened the service. Elser has taught math and science at Ennis High School for 30 years. He said all of the victims had been in his class.

"It's going to take a lot of time to heal this up," Elser said. "I guess we realized we are not immune to things like this."

On hand for the service was some of the family of Matthew Ortega, including his oldest brother, Greg Ortega.

He said Matthew had gone through surgery after taking a bullet through the ribs and out his back.

"They said he barely made it," Ortega said. "I'm just really glad he's alive."

He visited his brother at the hospital in Idaho Falls Saturday night. He said doctors are soon going to try to help Mathew take his first steps.

Ortega smiled when he talked about his brother's free spirit and how close the two had become the last few years. He said he already lost a brother in 1997 to a drowning accident.

"My mom couldn't take it if she lost another," Ortega said.

Back downtown, overlooking Main Street, Laurel McAtee stood on the steps of the Madison Valley Veterans Memorial. Officers were directing traffic and investigators were still sweeping the roadway.

"It's really beautiful, isn't it?" he asked. "What a horrific thing to happen to a little town like this."

# Chapter 12

## Do Not Do This Alone

The investigation team finished up by end-of-day Sunday. Officer Clark began another overnight shift, Sunday night into Monday morning. When that shift was almost done, one of his last duties was to assist Fire Chief Shawn Christensen with hosing down Main Street. This was the moment to complete this task. No one was downtown in the earliest hours of Monday morning. Everyone was still home sleeping or lying awake trying to figure out how to head into the workweek after the hell of this weekend. The business district was empty. It was time to rid Main Street and the residents of the most gruesome visual reminders of what happened here.

Together, Officer Clark and Chief Christensen ran the powerful fire hose, washing both the street and the sidewalk. The two men worked methodically and silently, completing their solemn task. The fire chief had been one of Jamie Roberts' closest friends and classmates. Torrents of water flooded along, picking up the usual gravel, cigarette butts, and leaves. But the murky water also washed away the dark, dried pools of their friends' blood.

The two proceeded down Main Street, not talking, alone with their own thoughts. They both saw, but did not mention, more delicate items carried away by the water. A ribbon once wrapped around a tattered bouquet. Greenery. Petals. Someone had laid wildflowers along the sidewalk where each victim had fallen. The two men didn't speak. They worked together. They completed a task that no one should have to do alone. That was enough for now.

# Chapter 13

## *The Work Begins*
## *Monday, June 16, 2003*

On Monday morning, a little over 48 hours after the shooting, the Ennis Town Hall was teeming with activity. The Town Clerk, Ginger Guinn, arrived early and stood outside, listening to the phone ringing incessantly inside. The parking lot was chaos too, with an inordinate number of cars and trucks jockeying for the last few spaces. Peering through the window in the door, Ginger could see a crowd of crime witnesses and concerned citizens crammed into the anteroom. Because Ginger and her husband, Andy, were members of the Madison Valley First Responders, they had served with the ambulance and at Madison Valley Hospital. Ginger had been living and reliving this event for more than two days when she arrived at work. Now the shooting would be the focus of her work for weeks to come. She took a deep breath and entered the building. The noise and the smell of over-brewed coffee hit her full force.

Ennis Police Officer Tom Tighe—a tall, dark-haired, usually jovial man—wore the worried countenance of a much older man. Several sheriff's deputies from Virginia City huddled together with Officer

Tighe, sharing information. Nearby, Mayor Ralph Hernandez was trying to find physical space in which he could assist in any way he could. The limited desks, tables, and chairs were, however, already over-occupied. The knot of town residents in the entry area would have been warmly welcomed on any other day. But today, they were only inadvertently hampering the work of the city staff, who desperately needed to convene and organize in private.

### ROBERTA R. ZENKER, Madison County Attorney

Promptly at 8:30 a.m., the door swung open and Madison County Attorney, Robert R. Zenker (Roberta R. Zenker[1]) swept in, ready to set up a makeshift office for crime witness interviews. As County Attorney, Roberta was under a deadline to prepare charging documents against George Harold Davis for presentation to the Circuit Judge of Madison County. It was her job to bring that man to trial for his heinous crimes.

She headed into the town hall's multipurpose room, claimed two metal folding chairs, and set up a temporary desk at a long conference table, arranging her notebooks, pens, and a recorder. Today, Roberta would begin gathering all legally relevant information and evidence in order to prosecute one of the biggest criminal cases in her career—and in the state's recent history. She'd had less than two hours of sleep in the past 24 hours, but she knew that time was always of the essence when a crime trail was hot. The information was still fresh in people's memories; her work had to begin today.

As she settled in, Roberta spoke with Ginger Guinn, the Town Clerk, and Susie Sprout, the Deputy Clerk. She filled them in on what to expect of this busy day, speaking with them gently, supportively.

Roberta knew that Ginger and Andy, as well as Susie, had all served with the ambulance crew. She knew both women came to work already taxed by the tragedy.

All three were longtime professional acquaintances, but Susie and Ginger rarely interacted with Roberta, whose office and court were in Virginia City. Roberta spoke kindly with both of them, acknowledging all that they had already been through. They would be seeing much more of each other in the coming days.

Thus began the long process of interviewing and questioning witnesses, as well as two of the survivors who were physically able to come to the Town Hall. Each witness was ushered in from the front room, one at a time, and Roberta guided them through the process of sharing their statements. Most were patrons of the Silver Dollar or the Claim Jumper, people who were present when the shooting happened. Others did not see the rampage, but they had interacted with Davis earlier in the evening and were willing to give whatever information they could. The shooting had shaken this town's foundation. Roberta took that awareness and respect into every interview.

Madison County sheriff's deputies sat at other tables in the same room generating lists of additional potential crime witnesses and other individuals who had seen or interacted with Davis. This list was pulled from Jason Klaumann's lengthy and detailed statement. By mid-morning, the chaos had transitioned into a steady din of conversation. The evidence-gathering system was up and running. New witnesses who arrived then were expediently guided to a separate line and, eventually, to Roberta's station. The phones still rang constantly in the front room, and doors swung open and slammed shut throughout the building every few seconds. The noise was constant, but everything soon had the feel of a well-oiled machine. The air was thick with carefully restrained panic, laced with focused intent.

Roberta's first interview was actually with a survivor: Trett Sutter. He came in on crutches. Roberta thought of her own son, only a few years younger. She helped Trett sit as comfortably as possible, then began her inquiry. Looking down, he spoke in a low and gentle voice. Trett provided a constrained and completely organized account of the evening. His recollections were focused, chronological, and surprisingly rich in detail.

Roberta was impressed with the young man's ability to lay out what had happened and amazed at how closely his accounting followed that of Jason's written statement. Roberta was trying to find a motive and make some logical sense of what had occurred. Trett went through his story, attempting to help the County Attorney with her goal, but he did not have an answer to that great question of "why." No one would.

Shortly after Trett gave his statement, Gavin Faulkner was able to come to the town hall as well. His mother, Maggi France, accompanied him. Gavin entered through the back door, awkwardly, trying to hold the door open for his mother despite being on crutches. Roberta again helped this young man sit as comfortably as possible. He was obviously emotionally affected by what had occurred. Roberta, Gavin, and his mother sat quietly for a moment, thinking of all the other survivors in hospitals all over the Rocky Mountain West. They thought of Jamie's family grieving in their home with their loved ones. After honoring them all with some reverent silence, Roberta began Gavin's interview.

AMY COOKSEY, Madison County Victim Advocate

Amy Cooksey, the Madison County Victim Advocate, also arrived at the Ennis Town Hall early Monday morning, summoned by her boss, Roberta Zenker. Amy had served as Victim Advocate for several years and had a decent idea of what would be required of her. She had cared for highly traumatized people before. Just not so many all at once and all harmed by the same violent crime. On her drive over to Ennis from Virginia City, she pondered what these people would need most. Roberta had given her a summary of the hell they'd been through. That summary was terrifying enough.

When she arrived at Town Hall, Amy took her place at a free corner of Roberta's conference table. The two began a sort of tag team with the witnesses. Roberta interviewed and questioned them, harvesting all the details necessary for prosecuting Davis. Then Roberta transferred the newly retraumatized person into Amy's comforting realm.

Between survivor care sessions, Amy made phone calls. She tracked down people whose names were repeatedly mentioned as the story of that night took shape. There were witnesses who had been in the bars earlier who might have information that could perhaps uncover Davis's elusive motive. One after another, Amy made her way through chains and chains of people who knew each other, who knew someone else who'd been there.

Over and over, she introduced herself over the phone: *This is Amy Cooksey, and I'm the Madison County, Fifth Judicial District Victim Advocate.* With that introduction, Amy connected with everyone she could possibly find who was affected by the shooting. Her low, soothing voice made it clear that she was someone they could trust and count on. One by one, she let each person know how she could help them through this time, and she let them know that the County Attorney would appreciate hearing any details they remembered about Davis, no matter how trivial they might think those details were.

Amy was not new to this process and had been particularly involved in sensitive cases involving abused children. She knew how to connect with traumatized people and understood the myriad ways people expressed themselves after experiencing a violent crime. Within a matter of hours, Amy had contacted Jamie's family, as well as all the survivors or their families or both. She had also reached out to people not directly injured, but clearly harmed emotionally. With each new contact, she made a note advising Zenker regarding whether the individual could possibly aid in building the case.

For days and weeks to come, Amy and Roberta worked side by side building that case. Roberta's goal was to lock up this man and prevent him from re-entering society forever. Amy's goal was to closely accompany the people he'd harmed, to notice how every step of the process might affect the witnesses, survivors, and their families, and to be there, always prepared to help them get through.

## ANGIE HOE (KUJULA) and GINGER POWERS

Ginger Powers remained in the hospital in Billings for two weeks. While she was there, her friend Angie, who worked and lived in Bozeman, regularly made the two-hour drive to visit and monitor her progress and recovery. Whenever Angie visited, other concerned friends from Ennis also stopped in to see how Ginger was doing and to give her their loving support. Angie began to feel a bit protective as she watched her friend force herself to rally physically every time someone new showed up in her room. Ginger tried so hard to show her appreciation to each kind and caring soul who made the long drive to see her.

During one of Angie's visits, two EMTs also showed up to say hi—they were part of the crew who had kept Ginger stabilized on her medical air flight from Ennis to Billings.

Angie was surprised at their visit; they weren't exactly Ennis locals! Ginger thought it was totally normal. "Oh, Angie, didn't I tell you? Since I've been here, those two men have visited me every day."

"Well, that is pretty incredible," Angie said.

"Do you think so?" asked Ginger, honestly puzzled.

"Well, I don't think they visit EVERY person they transport, do you?" Angie asked with a teasing giggle.

Angie realized then that her friend was not totally aware of her impact on people. Ginger brought out the best in everyone, just by being her quiet, gentle, caring self.

Having spent all that first Monday with Ginger, Angie missed her entire shift at First Security Bank of Bozeman. On Tuesday morning, she came in and went straight to her small desk in the bank's open work area on the first floor. One of her colleagues rushed over.

"Angie, how are you?" the woman asked, her big brown eyes full of concern. "How is your friend doing? How is *everyone* doing?"

"I didn't know you knew anything about what happened," Angie said.

"Oh, we've all been worried for you and your friend, ever since we read about it in the news and realized you were involved!"

Just then, their boss stopped by and said, "Angie, would you please come to my office in fifteen minutes?"

"Of course," Angie said, with a slight tightening in her stomach. She did call in the day before, and she did have sick days that she hadn't used. But she was worried there may have been some bad feelings about her taking the entire day off on such short notice. She busied herself tidying her desk. Then she swallowed hard, pushed back her chair, and began the walk down the carpeted path into the inner sanctum of the bank managers.

She cracked open her boss's door and waited to be asked in. The woman gestured at the chair in front of her desk, then she finished a phone conversation. Angie patiently waited in the chair.

Her boss hung up the phone, paused, and looked at Angie. She spread both of her hands flat on her desk and took a deep breath. "Angie, I want you to know that this bank completely supports you. We want you to know that you have an open door and complete freedom to come and go in the next few weeks to care for your friend in Billings. And to care for yourself and your own healing."

Angie physically sank into the chair, and tears began to flow. Not tears of sadness—she'd shed so many of those already in the last few days—but tears of utter appreciation for what her boss had just said to her. She was so touched by her employer's generosity.

"I can't thank you enough," Angie said. "I don't know how long Ginger will be in the hospital, but I'd like to be there with her, to help care for her and talk with her whenever she needs company."

"I can imagine you are just the person Ginger needs to talk to at this time," her boss said. Then they both stood, and Angie's boss came around her desk and embraced her, like a caring mother would. "We are here for you," she said. She clearly meant it.

Angie returned to her desk and began work for the day. Soon, her colleague stopped by her desk again, with a broad smile on her face.

"Everyone here decided to take up a donation. It's just this small amount, but we hope it might help all of your friends," she said and handed Angie a thick envelope. Then she quickly added, "We aren't done, either!" These people had never met Ginger nor any of the others, yet they were moved to make an effort to do something to help.

Later that day, Angie answered her personal cell phone and was startled to hear the voice of Amy Cooksey, the Victim Advocate.

"Oh, I'm surprised to hear from you," Angie said. "I can tell you how to get ahold of Ginger, if you want."

"No, Angie, I'm calling to check up on *you*," Amy replied.

Again, Angie felt her emotions well up; everything was so close to the surface these past few days. "I didn't know I would be on your radar," she said.

"Oh honey, you most certainly are on my radar, and I want you to know that I am here to help you with anything that gets overwhelming. I'll keep you up to date on the legal proceedings too."

Angie was touched by this. She didn't think she would be of interest to the Victim Advocate, but indeed she was. It was so affirming to hear that her trauma, as someone who saw the violence of that night, was also worth some focused care. How reassuring to realize there was someone who was willing to be a listening ear and provide legal insights too.

## ROBERTA ZENKER, AMY COOKSEY

Later that week, Roberta Zenker and Amy Cooksey drove together to Helena, Montana to meet with John Connor, the Montana Department of Justice (DOJ) Prosecution Services Bureau Chief. John would be participating in the prosecution of George Davis.

Roberta, who lived outside of Virginia City, picked up Amy in Dillon, and they began the two-hour drive north to Helena, to the State Capitol building. It was a beautiful drive through wide mountain valleys, ranchland, and winding canyons. Despite the heaviness of their task, they couldn't help but pause from their serious conversation to take in the green meadows speckled with herds of cows. Soft clouds kept the temperature in the 70s, and they left their windows open. They needed this—the drive, the fresh air. Soon they'd be indoors and focused on a difficult task for the rest of the morning.

They pulled into the parking area at the DOJ entrance, gathered their paperwork and briefcases, and headed into the ornate old capitol building. A statue of Jeanette Rankin, a Montanan and the first U.S. Congresswoman, looked down on them from her vantage point above the gallery. The two made their way to John's office. He stood to greet them and led them to the conference room, where they could spread out their documents.

The three worked closely, clarifying the heinous scene in John's mind. Roberta started the meeting with a carefully prepared, lengthy verbal description of how Davis progressed along the street, but she noticed that John looked puzzled. She realized he wasn't following the convoluted course of events. She and Amy resorted to using office supplies on the conference table to show the location of each victim, the fiend's path, and where each person fell.

As Roberta and Amy strove to provide an exact re-creation of the movements and path of the alleged perpetrator, they occasionally glanced outside to gather their thoughts. What a stark contrast: the stately buildings and the lush green lawn, and the horror they needed to describe in such vivid detail. The work was challenging, but this meeting forged a close connection between these three. They would work together on this prosecution for more than a year.

Once they concluded their meeting with John, Amy and Roberta headed to the historic business district to find a place for a late lunch before they returned to their offices in Virginia City. They got sandwiches and sat outside in the shade under century-old trees. It was a needed break from discussing the case; they talked about anything other than the shooting. They caught up as old friends on family, health, and summer plans and vacations. It felt almost normal.

Once they were back in Virginia City, in their own small offices in the county courthouse, Amy immediately returned to her work of following up with all the survivors. She got on the phone and started dialing. She needed to know how each one was doing, almost a week after the trauma. Jamie Roberts' family was at the top of her list. For the Clark family, for years thereafter, hers would be the name they mention as someone who truly helped to get them through this time.

She spent plenty of time calling all the other survivors too. No one was out of her concerned reach. Ginger and Isaiah were in Billings. She reached out to them and their families. She let them know that she would be the legal liaison to all the survivors and would share any new information with them as the Sheriff's Office and the County Attorney proceeded with their investigations and prosecution.

Jason Klaumann, who had already returned to his job and life in Salt Lake City, would completely depend on Amy for these legal updates. Jason had provided a highly detailed statement, the longest on record in the case file, and it would become the backbone of the entire legal case.

It didn't take long for Amy to realize that these young people needed some ongoing professional mental health support as well as the more general resources she could offer. She connected with Jim Deming, a psychologist in Bozeman, who was willing to provide free counseling to the victims of the shooting. She also spoke with the wider group of survivors, witnesses, and loved ones, letting them all know about the resources available to them in Madison County. Throughout the next few weeks, Amy made personal contact with 39 secondary victims—the survivors and witnesses of the Ennis shooting and their loved ones.

After only one week, the town of Ennis was already forging a path forward with its own particular wealth of human kindness. That loving kindness would sustain and unite every witness, survivor and family member affected by the shooting, for years to come.

**Endnote:**

[1]Roberta R. Zenker, author of *TransMontana, a Memoir of Transformation in Body, Mind and Spirit (Independently published 2012).*

# Chapter 14

## *Farewell to Jamie*
## *Wednesday, June 17, 2003*

More than 650 people flowed into the new Madison Valley Rural Fire District building on Highway 287. When the main parking lot was full, vehicles overflowed into the surrounding fields in neat rows and even more carefully parked all along both sides of the highway. This multitude of respectfully dressed citizens walked whatever distance was necessary to attend Jamie Roberts' funeral. It was yet another beautiful summer day, and a cool breeze comforted them all.

That week, the volunteer members of the Madison Valley Rural Fire District had converted the entire building into an appropriate and welcoming setting for a funeral of this size. The town of Ennis always chose its funeral locations thoughtfully. The rodeo grounds had hosted the send-off of several well-known citizens during fair weather months. The high school gym was often used for the services of well-loved citizens during the winter. Of course, every single church had hosted countless memorials over the years. But when loved ones expected a huge crowd, these other facilities were considered. With Jamie, given his own service as a firefighter, it only made sense that the fire hall and his colleagues there would host his send-off.

The fire department volunteers had been at work since Monday, preparing the meeting room and fire hall for this. They'd set up hundreds of folding chairs and cleared the perimeter for the anticipated standing room overflow. In the greatest of ironies, the room would inevitably exceed its set capacity for fire safety. No one cared. At the north wall, they set up an artful dais draped with a white cloth, upon which they'd hefted a snowmobile, draped in flower garlands. Most present knew that this would have pleased Jamie, who was a passionate snowmobiler. Many were lucky enough to have memories of enjoying that pastime with him, and they teared up as soon as they walked in and saw the snowmobile.

Reverend Jean Johnson of the Madison Valley Presbyterian Church stood near the front of the hall, waiting to speak to the grief, sadness, shock, and anger present in the packed fire hall. She was as prepared as she could be, to give her all to her community.

People entered quietly, everyone seeking out family and friends. What a heavy day for Jamie's family and everyone closest to him. But that core family group smiled in thanks to the crowd of guests. They felt incredible gratitude for such an outpouring of support. People filled all the available seats and then the standing room at the back and sides of the hall. The flow of community members finally reached a lull, and there was a moment of solemn anticipation.

Heads turned as Joe Dickinson, Kenny Shirley Jr., Mike Sprout, Spencer Noack, Shawn Christensen, Cooper Taylor, Mike McKitrick, Cody Covas, and Jason Bjorngaard, the pallbearers, entered with their precious burden. These strong young men brought Jamie's casket in through the wide-open doors, and up through the huge and silent gathering, to the waiting dais.

Every person present felt their throats tighten. Eyes burned with sad and angry tears. Husbands and wives wrapped their arms around each other's shoulders; mothers and fathers hugged their children close to their chests. Young people clustered together and held hands. All drew close to someone, and no one stood alone. Three survivors were able to attend: Isaiah Crowley, Gavin Faulkner, and Trett Sutter, and their families. Mike Carroll, Ginger Powers, and Matthew Ortega were still in critical care in far-flung hospitals, but their family members were present to represent them and report to them.

The pallbearers set the casket down, and each man sat down with loved ones in the first few rows. Silence settled over the crowd. Then Reverend Jean stepped forward. She began her service with a powerful declaration: "It isn't supposed to be, that parents bury their children!" Speaking on behalf of the Clark family, she railed against the horrible disorder of this tragedy, this nightmare still happening to Doug and Sharon, Jamie's sister Katy, his wife Kandi, and little Kyra.

Throughout her message, Reverend Jean repeatedly asked the Lord to "grant us rest!" She clearly felt the hearts of all present, and honestly addressed their weariness and brokenness, their shattered sense of safety, vigilant tears, and constant shock. This was her community's reality now. There was no way to change that. Her best prayer in such a moment was for rest—for occasional moments of escape from this new state of fear, grief, and anger.

Reverend Jean talked about Jamie as someone who knew him. This was no stock sermon clinging to standard Bible verses in lieu of personal knowledge of the person being laid to rest. She described

Jamie as "a good citizen, a good husband, son, and father," and she went on to describe him in far more specific and precious terms. She celebrated the exuberant life that he led, calling him a Teddy Bear with a winning smile. He was the guy who performed at his own homecoming dance as a "Not Quite Ready for Nashville" karaoke singer—those who were lucky enough to have witnessed that antic, broke out in a wave of gentle laughter. Reverend Jean talked about Jamie's love for his dog, Berkeley, and how he played on an old typewriter with his daughter, and at some point, she quipped, "He is probably cranking up heaven's Polaris at this very moment, to go sledding around heaven's peaks!"

Reverend Jean knew Jamie. Any present who had not known him well, gleaned a deep understanding from her message, from such cherished details about who he was and what he meant to his family and the town. The reverend also made room for powerful exhortations and encouragement for everyone in the room, summoning them all:

"I challenge and urge each of you here today to become better and stronger than every evil and any hurt! I challenge you to make your goodness broader than our valley, higher than our mountains! I challenge you all to turn evil into good, to turn hurt into healing, to turn anger at one into compassion for each other. By this, the loss of Jamie will not be in vain but will one day be the source of new life, renewed strength, and new hope!"

Reverend Jean had conducted funerals for other young people who had passed too early; it was not her first time dealing with such a painful grief. This middle-aged woman brought her experience as a spiritual leader, along with her warm heart, personal strength, forth-right honesty, love, and strong faith, to respond to the profound loss:

"I stand before you today with a feeling deep down in the pit of my stomach that anything I say must seem very trivial...there is no loss so striking, so humbling, so tragic, so full of grief as the loss of our children...the way in which Jamie's life was lost multiplies the family's grief, and our grief too. The loss of Jamie's life under these circumstances is its own unique kind of tragedy. Our minds race back to memories, times spent with Jamie, and our minds race ahead to all the things Jamie will never do again, to experiences we will never have with him, to joyous future moments filled with Jamie's practical jokes, lost to us, forever.

"It isn't supposed to be like this, one of our kids, one of our Ennis kids—his life ended by a senseless, illogical act of violence. Jamie's tragic death brings us here today and weighs heavily upon us, a young life so rich in promise, cut short. A young life, so closely bound to ours, abruptly ended. We come together to express our shared loss. We come to pay tribute to Jamie, who touched our lives in varying degrees in different ways."

Reverend Jean called on everyone to channel all their love and loss into the immense challenge now before them. They must stand together. She clearly named what the community was already doing: growing closer, fonder, and more tender and understanding toward one another. She closed with a call to prayer for the survivors and the community:

"With deep affection, loving God, we remember Jamie. Keep all our memories fresh in our hearts. Help us to share with each other the moments of joy and celebration shared with Jamie. We thank you for the gift of Jamie's life. We thank you for love given and love received, defeats mastered, and tasks well done, a brief life lived with joy. We thank you for all graces of soul and character which endeared Jamie to us and fulfilled your purposes for him. Grant us peace, O God, as we surrender him to you. We pray for all our wounds and wounded. The survivors, wounded in body, all of us wounded in spirit. Mighty and merciful God, you sent Jesus the Christ to heal broken lives. We praise you for the skill of our doctors, nurses and EMTs. For the blessing of technology used to heal. We claim your promises of wholeness as we pray for the injured and their families:

*Matt Ortega, Mike Carroll, Ginger Powers, Isaiah Crowley, Gavin Faulkner, Trett Sutter"*

She spoke each name, letting each one hang in the air a while, letting the community hold each person in their hearts. Then she closed her prayer and invited three of the pallbearers—Michael Sprout, Kenny Shirley, and Cooper Taylor—to share their memories.

Michael stood from his seat and headed to the microphone. A quiet man with a gentle voice, he spoke of his lifelong friendship with Jamie and their shared outdoor interests. He reminded everyone, "You all knew Jamie Roberts' truck!" This prompted much-needed laughter. People in Ennis certainly did know each other's vehicles. He went on to extol Jamie's work ethic and his reliability as a kind and generous friend. When Michael finished, Kenny stood and spoke. He told the gathering:

"Jamie often said he was not scared to die. I believe Jamie truly was ready, in some way, to die. That leaves just us, his friends and family, and this entire community, who are not ready for him to die. You all should know that Jamie's motto was "NO FEAR!" That is what my friend embraced his whole well-lived, short life."

Cooper then approached the podium. A man who came from a family of actors and writers, Cooper was a renowned Hollywood stunt man and actor. How had he connected with Jamie? Three generations and two branches of Cooper's family had their roots in the Madison Valley. So Cooper and Jamie were just a couple of Ennis guys who enjoyed outdoor pastimes together. Cooper shared memories from a 20-year friendship, recalling going to school together, and then admiring Jamie for the man he became—a fine carpenter, a family man, and an incredible friend:

> "Jamie had so much pride in his beautiful daughter, Kyra. Jamie was kind and caring and took care of everyone. Jamie literally saved my life during a snowmobiling adventure when he noticed that I had somehow gotten all of my clothes wet. He changed our course, and led us to a cabin, and started a fire, so I could dry my clothes and warm up! I truly believe that Jamie saved my life that day!"

Sharon Clark, Jamie's mother, listened attentively to her son's young friends. As each man spoke, she became increasingly physically distressed. Amy Cooksey was seated nearby, and she was well familiar with the signs that a person might faint. Sharon's breathing was shallow, and she'd turned noticeably pale. Amy quickly made her way to Sharon's side, and Sharon glanced at her with relief in her eyes.

Amy physically held Sharon up and whispered to her. As Sharon began to collapse, Amy supported her body, allowing the two of them to drop to the ground together, smoothly and unharmed. In a few minutes, Sharon was able to stand and return to her seat.

As Cooper finished sharing his memories, Sharon was back in her seat, but still felt shaky. She wanted something to be said on behalf of the family, to thank the community for coming, but she clearly didn't feel she was up to that task. She whispered to Amy, asking her to speak on her behalf. Amy gave Sharon a gentle nod, made her way to the podium, and began:

"My name is Amy Cooksey, and I am standing here at this moment, for the family of Jamie Roberts. Doug, Sharon, and Katy Clark; Kandi Popp and Kyra Roberts; and Jamie's Grandpa and Grandma Bjorngaard and Grandma Beulah Clark are so immensely comforted to feel the loving support coming from this huge contingent of the Ennis and the Madison Valley community. They want to thank each and every one of you for being here, and for being in Jamie's life."

As Amy left the podium, a collective inhalation and heavy sigh filled the room. All of the more than 600 souls in the fire hall thought tenderly of Jamie's parents, his sister, his wife and daughter, and his grandparents. Reverend Jean returned to the podium and let the prayerful silence extend itself for a while.

Then she took a breath and guided everyone back into the here and now. This moment, itself, was a practice in how the community would carry on from that day forward. Everyone there, in coming months and years, would walk a path that led in and out of intense moments of deep grief and then back into the most ordinary tasks of daily life. In this case, in this moment of deep grief, it was now time for lunch.

The fire hall hosted the luncheon, and Madison Valley Bank provided the food. The bank had cancelled its own anniversary party, previously scheduled for this day. Then they donated all the food to the memorial. Jamie's memorial service concluded, and lunch began.

A din of chatter soon echoed throughout the fire hall as the community shared warm greetings, food, and memories. Everyone found a chance to embrace someone not seen for a while. Some intentionally sought out folks with whom perhaps cross words had been spoken in the past, both parties now eager to put petty conflicts aside with a warm embrace.

People gently jockeyed for contact with each of Jamie's family members, as well as the survivors and their families. They were all herded from one loving group to another and offered anything they needed right then—food, hugs, a chair—and anything they would need in the future. Those who had not been directly affected by the shooting made their presence known to those who had been utterly devastated. There was a common purpose, unspoken, but crystal clear: *Jamie's family, and the survivors and their families, must be assured with absolute certainty that they are not alone.*

119

As the lunch came to a close, the mood shifted once more, and loved ones gathered to begin the vehicle procession to the cemetery. People began to quietly and respectfully file out of the fire station, heads downcast, though often glancing up to make silent eye contact with friends. They felt such a bond, such unanimity, in this sadness laced with endurance. All the members of the great extended family that is the Town of Ennis and the Madison Valley exited the fire hall into the bright sunlight. They walked arm in arm to their vehicles. They made their thoughtful departure, loaded into their trucks and cars, and set off for the cottonwood-shaded cemetery where Jamie would be laid to rest.

Traffic leading in and out of Ennis was stopped for half an hour to allow for the procession from the fire hall to the Madison Valley Cemetery at the south side of town. The procession, composed mostly of pickup trucks, stretched more than a mile and progressed with a slow and steady solemnity down Main Street.

Every flag in town was at half mast, and as the procession passed by businesses that hadn't been able to close for the day, employees and shop owners came outside to say farewell and pay their last respects to Jamie. Several small businesses had closed, including the Silver Dollar Saloon. A small sign was posted on its door, which read "Closed for the Funeral," and a bouquet of flowers sat on the windowsill.

At the cemetery, some of the vehicles split from the procession and respectfully headed home, honoring the family's privacy as they laid Jamie to rest. Then, Reverend Jean led Jamie's family and close friends through their final goodbye.

After the funeral, there was a small gathering at Doug and Sharon's home. Constantly attentive and caring, Amy attended both the funeral and this gathering at the Clarks' house. There she overheard people asking who she was, as she wasn't exactly a local. She lived in Dillon, about 90 miles northwest of Ennis. At one point, Amy overheard Doug Clark's answer to this repeated question: "That's Amy Cooksey. She's the newest member of our family."

# ~ ARTIFACTS ~

*A Community Grieves and Cares for its Own*

# Letter to the Editor

## Melinda Merrill, *The Madisonian*; June 18, 2003

*Melinda Merrill, a business owner and mother of four daughters, who were the ages of the young people harmed by the shooting, felt compelled to research and write a comprehensive acknowledgement of all the local heroes of that terrible night.*

I would like to extend a heartfelt salute and thank you to all the professionals who were involved with the shooting in Ennis. What a testament it is to the professionals, local and regional, both paid and volunteer personnel that came from all over a large geographical area to help our small community...how much we owe these people... how can we ever begin to express our gratitude?

Information provided from the dispatch log shows that the night shift officer, Dave Clark, traveled fourteen miles and arrived from Virginia City in ten minutes of the call that confirmed a shooting had occurred. Our local Ennis Officer, Tom Tighe, received "the call" a few minutes later at home and arrived in less than eight minutes from more than twenty miles away. Sheriff Schenck, who was off duty at the time, arrived from his home in Ennis at the same time as

Officer Tighe. This placed three officers at the scene of the shooting within sixteen minutes of "the call."

The officers immediately began working to help the wounded, secure the scene and secure the hospital where the victims were being transported. The team then began searching for the shooter. Within one hour, officers, both on and off duty, arrived from all parts of the state to aid and assist.

The 911 phone lines were inundated with calls, and the local dispatcher did a tremendous job of handling all incoming calls while at the same time dispatching ambulances, officers, alerting hospital staff, etc.—all simultaneously.

We are fortunate in this community that Ennis High School requires "First Responder" (training) as a graduation requirement. The Ennis Alumni on the scene at the time of the shooting immediately began giving first aid, possibly helping to make the difference between life and death.

The ambulance crew from our hometown responded and were on the scene within four minutes of receiving "the call." Overall, there were eleven Ennis EMTs that responded; three EMTs with an ambulance from Sheridan; one EMT from Virginia City (who drove over personally to help); plus an ambulance and crew from Bozeman. There were two helicopter life flights and one fixed-wing flight here in Ennis taking the victims to Billings and Idaho Falls—pilots, medical personnel; doctors, nurses, technicians, and staff from the Madison Valley Hospital...all working to save lives. I thank God for and appreciate every single one of you.

The Madison County Law Enforcement chose to network with other departments across the area, bringing in the Montana Division of Criminal Investigations into Ennis. The Gallatin County Sheriff, Sheriff Cashell, volunteered three crime scene detectives and himself to help secure Main Street in Ennis and help with the investigation.

The Montana Highway Patrol not only had officers on the scene, controlling traffic and searching the area for the shooter, but also sent an expert to do a "total stations and mapping" for the crime scene.

Chaplain Warren Hiebert, the southwest regional Chaplain for the State of Montana, has spent days here consoling, counseling and comforting those involved.

After the initial response, still volunteers came from all over, to continue to help our small community…most of them volunteers giving of their time with immense caring compassion. On Saturday morning, EMTs from the RAE Fire Department, and also from the Amsterdam Fire Department, arrived in Ennis to give relief to the Ennis Crew, handling the calls for the next 24 hours to allow our EMTs to get some much-needed rest.

The Madison Valley Search and Rescue Squad and members of the Madison Valley Fire Department continued for two more days, twenty-four hours a day, assisting with traffic control and helping as needed.

On the day of Jamie Roberts' funeral, there were volunteers from Fort Ellis, Belgrade, Big Sky, Sourdough RAE, Amsterdam and Belgrade Rural Fire Departments that again came to cover for our local men and women, so that they might attend the service and be with family.

Again… how can we even begin to express our gratitude to our "neighbors" for their concern and help. I am sure that I have left out some unsung hero, but be it known… we are forever grateful.

Tragedy struck our small town of a thousand, and our lives will be forever changed. However, we can stand proud of our community for its response. We will always be indebted to these fine professionals that gave of their time and energy. Thank you is not enough... we salute you... we appreciate you... we are proud of you... we support you... we thank you... may God bless each one of you and keep you safe, now and always.

∼

## Editorial
Editorial Staff, *The Madisonian*; June 18, 2003

Our heartfelt thoughts and prayers go out to the victims of this last weekend's tragic incident that took place in our Ennis community, to their families and to their friends and acquaintances, all of whom have been touched by these events.

Sincerely,

The Madisonian Staff

∼

## Letter to the Editor
Jan Coffman and Carrie Coffman-Smith,
*The Madisonian*; June 18, 2003

### IN MEMORY OF JAMIE ROBERTS

A Memorial Fund has been set up at First Madison Valley Bank in Ennis for anyone wishing to make a donation in memory of Jamie, that will go to his 3-year-old daughter, Kyra Nicole Roberts.

Our thoughts and prayers for the Clark family, Kandi and Kyra are with you in this time of loss.

We miss you, Jamie, and you will never be forgotten by looking at Kyra.

Memories are forever,
Love, Jan Coffman, Carrie Coffman-Smith

∽

## Column: Around the Wood Stove
Gail Banks, *The Madisonian*; June 18, 2003

*A regular columnist for* The Madisonian, *Gail Banks, dedicated that week's column to honoring those harmed by the shooting.*

Can't send out enough sympathy and compassion to the Ennis area for their sorrow and grief during this week after the terrible shooting incident. Nothing can be said to the Ennis community to help with their sorrow. Except for the many prayers for them all the wounded and healing, the lost friend, and their many families and friends. How can any sense of whys be brought to this kind of thing?

∽

## Public Notice
*The Madisonian*; June 18, 2003

### Grief Counseling

As most members of the Ennis community are aware, on the early morning hours of June 14 at approximately 2:10 a.m., a shooting occurred in the downtown area resulting in a total of seven people being shot, one fatally. As a result of this tragedy, the Town of Ennis will be holding a town meeting at the Ennis High School on Thursday, June 19, at 7:00 p.m. The purpose of this town meeting will be to provide grief counseling for anyone in need.

A memorial fund for the family of Jamie Roberts has been set up at the First Madison Valley Bank. An account has also been set up for all victims' families at Valley Bank.

We appreciate the members of our community who really made a difference during this traumatic time. I would like to name a few specifically, the Ennis Ambulance Volunteers, the Madison Valley Hospital Staff, the Ennis Pharmacy, the staff at the Sportsman's Lodge, the Montana Highway Patrol, the Madison County Sheriff's Department, the Madison County Dispatch, and the assistance we received from Gallatin County Sheriff's Department in processing this difficult crime scene. I am extremely grateful for the way this community has come together in this time of crisis to offer their support.

~

## Letter to the Editor: Thank-You Card Section

The Clark Family, *The Madisonian*; July 3, 2003

We would like to extend our heartfelt thanks to everyone who came by the house with food, beverages, cards, sent flowers and words of encouragement. The outpouring of love, concern and affection by our friends, family and the whole community has been phenomenal.

Special thanks to Mike Stecker, Jean Johnson, Tanya Fortner, Jan Coffman, Carrie Coffman Smith, Rob and Brenda Arrotta, the Madison Valley Fire Department, First Madison Valley Bank and Harrington's Pepsi Company. We would also like to thank each and every one of you who put money into Kyra Roberts Memorial Fund.

Jamie was an outstanding young man and he will be terribly missed by not only his family and close friends, but the whole community. Our prayers continue for the other six survivors, their families and friends, and we hope that they will continue to get better each and every day. We are all truly blessed to live in such a wonderful community.

Doug, Sharon & Katy Clark
Kyra Roberts, Kandi Popp
Grandma and Grandpa Bjorngaard
Grandma Beulah Clark
& All the Rest of Jamie's Family,
God Bless You All

## Special Sale Notice

*The Madisonian;* July 3, 2003

**FOR SALE**
**Registered 1992 Appaloosa Gelding**
**$1,800 ~ Trail or Ranch Horse**

ALL PROCEEDS WILL BENEFIT THE VICTIMS
OF JUNE 14, 2003

CB RANCH
682-4608

This ranch is owned by Chris and Sandra Vanderlans.

∾

## Letter to the Editor

Roundup Rodeo Committee, *The Madisonian*; July 3, 2003

*The Rodeo Committee of Roundup, Montana—a small town over 200 miles away from Ennis—wrote a heartfelt letter and made a touching offer of financial help. Their sense of solidarity was palpable; all of small-town Montana felt for their own when they heard what happened in Ennis.*

Dear Community Members:

This is absolutely the most difficult letter we've ever had to encounter, but we find it completely necessary to try to respond in some way to the horrendous losses you all have had to experience and will continue to experience.

As a small, tight-knit community ourselves our hearts ache at the thought of the abuse your community has suffered purely for being the kind and generous people we know you to be. Like you, we pride ourselves in opening our community, our homes, and even our hearts to those moving in or even just passing through. We just never even hesitate to think that this warmth we offer would be received in such a bastardly manner. It's unthinkable, unforgiveable, and sadly, unforgettable!

Though we have no way of lessening your anguish, we hope to offer some comfort and support not only for your community but also to the families of the youngsters so dreadfully affected. We want you to know that our hearts and our prayers are with each of you as recovery continues to unfold.

Additionally, we commit to provide financial assistance to the seven families, clearly financially stricken, by donating our rodeo committee receipt from the 50/50 drawing to be held over our July 3rd and 4th Rodeo.

We plan to forward these funds directly to the Ennis Rodeo Committee but do intend to notify you as to our daily progress.

Though the resulting dollars may be a drop in the bucket, the underlying heartfelt thoughts behind them are boundless. We wish you peace and comfort in the days to come.

# Chapter 15

## *Fourth of July 2003*

During the first three weeks after the shooting, the town of Ennis had already shown that it would survive intact. Yes, everyone was still reeling from losing Jamie and caring for the six wounded survivors. Yet the community was confronting its first big decision regarding how they would carry on. *Should they still host their usual July Fourth extravaganza? The parade and regional rodeo that drew thousands?* The answer was a brisk and tenacious "yes." The rodeo committee and competitors, the Main Street shop owners, and countless volunteers bucked up and braced themselves to prepare for the crowds. They committed to dedicating every event that holiday weekend to Jamie, his family, and the survivors.

Every organization and business in the town of Ennis participated. The line-up of events included, as always, the preliminary July 3 qualifying rodeo, the Fire Department's Pancake Breakfast first thing on July 4, the regionally famous Ennis Rodeo Parade at 10:00 a.m., food and festivities all afternoon at multiple locations, and then the Ennis Fourth of July Rodeo at 3:00 p.m. Finally, at the end of the day, everyone would head over the mountain pass to take in the fireworks display in Virginia City.

On the evening of July 3, the festivities began. Fans packed into the two wooden, slightly splintery grandstands on either side of the rodeo arena and watched young rodeo champions compete to qualify for the next day's main rodeo event. The competitors came from rodeo circuits all over the U.S., but a fair number were local favorites. The sun set over the Madison Range as the audience cheered their favorite cowboys and cowgirls on toward victory. It almost felt like any other year. Though even the out-of-towners knew by now what had happened here barely a month before, that knowledge didn't dampen spirits. If anything, the feeling of celebration heightened; it felt important to prove that nothing could be ruined by the tragedy. Folks cheered for the competitors all the louder.

As always, early on Independence Day morning, the Madison Valley Rural Fire District held its annual fundraising pancake breakfast. All the local volunteer firefighters served up breakfast to the community and any rodeo guests who woke up early enough. The locals carried the quiet knowledge that, only a few weeks earlier, they'd gathered in this same building to remember Jamie and surround his family with love.

Outwardly, the fire hall was back to its usual pancake breakfast set up with long rows of folding tables and folding chairs. The food was offered along one side of the hall, and the line moved through with grateful anticipation. Laughter and the sweet aromas of maple syrup, pancakes, sausage, and coffee filled the hall. Cars streamed in and out of the parking lot, which had again overflowed into the nearby field and along the highway. Families tumbled out of cars and pickups in happy anticipation.

At the propped-open door, two men stood side by side. They were older, longtime volunteer firefighters, taking a moment to rest from welcoming, steering, cooking, serving, and cleaning up. They surveyed the scene and chatted.

"Looks like a bigger turnout than last year."

"Sure does."

"Well, it's just good we can do something for Jamie's little girl."

The two were quiet a moment, likely considering the ramifications of the MVRFD donating all its fundraiser proceeds to the trust fund for Kyra Roberts. The decision had been unanimous.

"Right thing to do."

"Indeed."

"Back to work then?"

"Yeah, better get cracking!"

"Eggs, that is!"

All Jamie's fire department comrades donned brave smiles, flipped pancakes, and cooked bacon and sausage. At the end of the morning, they tallied the cash and locked it up for deposit on Monday morning into Kyra Roberts' trust account at First Madison Valley Bank.

Once their hunger was sated, local families and friends and carloads of tourists left the fire hall and headed downtown to secure good vantage points for watching the Ennis Fourth of July Rodeo Parade. How could it be that only three weeks earlier, a few of the shooting survivors had run for their lives down this same street? Matthew Ortega had run up the stairs alongside the West of the Madison building. Now, in broad daylight, tourists shopped for t-shirts and souvenirs in that store. A joyful crowd lined up in front of the building and every other shop and bar on Main Street. Families with young ones in tow jockeyed to get as close as possible to the highway shoulder, so they could be the first to catch candy tossed from floats.

Business owners milled about outside their shops, taking in the growing crowd. They called to each other over the din, discussing the turnout:

--*Lot more people this year!*

--*I overheard some tourists wondering how we could pull it off this time.*

--*Oh, nothing can keep us down!*

--*Have you heard every one of the survivors are back home now?*

--*That so?*

--*Yeah, that's the power of our prayers.*

As usual there were more garish red, white, and blue outfits than should ever appear in one place at the same time. Young children surged out into the streets while cautious parents tried to rein them in, visualizing the large horses who would soon occupy the same real estate. But the children were drawn by the promise of all the candy that would soon be bouncing along the hot blacktop. The happy, anticipatory crowd was like that of any other around the country on this day, and the heat was mounting along with the pitch of excitement. The crowd was a jolly, ten-to-thirty-people-deep on both sides of Main. Many locals had parked pickup trucks on either side of the street the night before. The truck beds now held camping chairs and happy family groups.

Then at 10:00 a.m., as it had every year since 1950, the Ennis Chamber of Commerce launched the annual Rodeo Parade. Trumpets in a marching band blasted the first chord in a rousing song, and every neck craned, all heads turned north to catch the first glimpse of the band. Children and their parents, young adults, grandparents, friends, strangers, and visitors, a wider community of several thousand, were rapt with attention for an American tradition.

Yet, between floats and dance numbers and clown routines, locals met and, over clasped hands, shared news of the recovering young people. They smiled to hear that everyone was home and recovering well. So thankful. Yet those smiles covered a deep worry and continued sadness for Jamie's family and all the lasting scars, both physical and emotional. So short a time ago, there was blood where folding chairs now sat. This same street, now teeming with people, was where a lone madman shattered the hopes, plans, and expectations of so many young people.

How did the town pull it off? It was a choice. The festivities today showed to the residents, the visitors, and the world, that evil would not be allowed to take up residence here. Strength, hope, and promise would prevail.

To the south, the parade grandstand was set up in front of the First Madison Valley Bank Building at the middle of the parade route.

This provided a lookout for the crucial business of parade float competition, for naming the winning floats and honorees. Mary Oliver, the bank's COO, was the Presenter and Master of Ceremonies, as she had been for many years. She was also the one who spearheaded establishing the trust account for Jamie's daughter.

Mary announced: "The Grand Marshal of the parade this year is Larry Gleason. Larry and his wife Ruby own our local Dairy Queen. Their son, Brad, was a rodeo champion." A tall cowboy on an even taller horse, Larry looked almost regal as he rode down Main Street. Mary continued, "Larry Gleason is this year's Grand Marshal in honor of his decades-long service to the Ennis Rodeo Association as a rodeo clown—charged with the safety of the rodeo's participants. He and Ruby have been Ennis residents and highly respected community volunteers since 1949!"

Here, leading the parade was a local business owner and horseman, someone tied to both the town and ranching communities. Larry would be a perfect choice as Parade Grand Marshal any year, but this year his presence was even more powerful. Ennis was proud of its ranching history, and yet a single ranch hand had tarnished that pride. Perhaps more than any other public celebration that summer, the Fourth of July Parade was a chance to reclaim that pride. Larry led the way.

Throughout the crowd and the parade itself there were so many strong, handsome cowboys. Their simple presence reminded everyone of the true identity of ranchers and ranch life. These were men one could trust, men who could be relied upon, and men who took care of friends and neighbors. Their presence helped the community remember those core values.

The parade also featured the various 4H clubs in and around the valley, including the Cameron Longhorns and the McAllister Mountaineers. Small calves and sheep zig-zagged down the street, with even smaller cowboys and cowgirls herding them along or walking them with halters and rope. Yes, the traditions of this ranching community would remain solid. No single person could shake that honor and pride.

The Ennis Community Children's School soon passed through with their own herd of youngsters on tricycles. Young, energetic teachers attempted to keep that herd going in the right direction. Many locals in the crowd teared up watching those little ones. They thought of how many of the young adults affected by the shooting had attended this very school as preschoolers themselves, back when the school was first founded. The innocence of the children in the parade only heightened everyone's awareness of the town's shattered innocence. This awareness no doubt released another jet stream of loving thoughts and healing prayers for each of the young survivors, wherever they were.

The music was constant, from brass bands to banjo, to recorded hip hop beats. The heat was more or less manageable, and from all appearances, the crowd was happy. As the float entries dwindled towards the end, a truck pulling a large flatbed trailer appeared. On it were the past high school classmates of Jamie Roberts: Cammie Goetze, Stephanie Flavell, Jason Klaumann, Cooper Taylor, Joe Dickinson, and others, along with Kandi and Kyra. A large, colorful banner proclaimed, "In Honor of Jamie Roberts, NOT TO BE FORGOTTEN." The young people threw candy to expectant children's hands, but as the float progressed onward, a quieter atmosphere descended on the crowd.

As the float passed by the marquee, Mary Oliver announced, "Finally we have a very special entry this year. This float hosts the 1994 graduating class of Ennis High School, commemorating the brief but very memorable life of Jamie Roberts. This community lost Jamie in a tragedy which took his life too soon, in June of this year. Anyone who would care to make a donation to benefit Jamie's young daughter may do so at the special account set up at First Madison Valley Bank." She went on to describe the account at Valley Bank also set up to benefit "all the other young people who were injured in that tragedy."

The float triggered a wave of questions among any out-of-towners who weren't yet clear about what had happened here. *Who was Jamie? What exactly happened?* One by one, nearby locals chimed in to answer those questions soberly, yet with pride. Yes, that happened here. But no, it was not about to define or in any way change the nature of our town.

As always, all bars on Main Street, including the Silver Dollar, extended their real estate into the roadway through ropes and stanchions, outlining additional patio space. Here their customers could enjoy a somewhat exclusive area in which to enjoy adult beverages and watch the parade.

The Claim Jumper, the Silver Dollar, and the Long Branch saloons were hopping and spilling their happy thirsty patrons onto the sidewalks and the parking areas in the makeshift "corrals." Those VIP enclosures brimmed with tourists and a cadre of locals bound together by the tragedy. The very act of carrying forward with joyful interaction was a defiant stance against the horror perpetrated by one man.

Meanwhile, at the south end of town, the Ennis Lion's Club began preparations for their massive hamburger barbecue, soon to feed the hordes in the Lion's Club Park. As the parade wound down, families headed to the park. Mothers and fathers spread blankets on the grass, and children raced around, occasionally taking a break from playtime to eat a hamburger or hot dog. For the Lion's Club volunteers, this day was only a warm-up. Tomorrow, the fifth of July, they would cater an equally important meal. But first, everyone's attention was focused on today's main event: the Ennis Fourth of July Rodeo.

As the heat of the afternoon mounted, families made their way to the dirt parking area at the rodeo grounds and filed toward the ticket booth. The line was long and, as they waited, folks connected with acquaintances they hadn't seen in a while. Lighthearted conversations quickly evolved into more meaningful inquiries, peppered with many thoughtful pauses. People were quick to give a supportive hug or shoulder squeeze to each other.

The tickets had seat rows and numbers, and the out-of-towner hordes mostly headed to the right, and locals headed to the bleachers on the left. All filed into the bleachers and prepared for the competitive fun, excitement, sweat, and sun, along with some patriotic camaraderie. Soon a hush wove through the mass of warm bodies, and faces turned toward the grandstand with anticipation.

The announcer welcomed the crowd and shared a few brief histories of the young rodeo contestants who would be competing. Then he introduced a lovely blonde cowgirl who stood on the stage behind him. She removed her hat as the announcer handed the microphone to her. The sun caught her golden hair. There was complete silence, and a momentous "whoosh" as hundreds of hats were removed, and people stood up in unison.

*O say can you see*
*By the dawn's early light*
*What so proudly we hailed*
*At the twilight's last gleaming?*

The cowgirl was young, but her crystalline voice was surprisingly rich. It was a haunting *a cappella* rendition that brought tears and thoughtful silence to even the rowdiest of revelers. Beyond the rodeo grounds, the sound system carried her lovely voice throughout the entire north end of town. Everyone thought for a moment, not only of the country's founding, but also of their own values—which had been threatened so profoundly so recently.

*O'er the land of the free...*
*And the home of the brave.*

The brave family of Jamie Roberts, the brave survivors and their families, and the brave citizens of Ennis who would not allow anything to change their town. Throughout the crowd, cowboys redonned their hats; many paused for a moment, hiding behind hat brims to brush away tears.

The announcer took the microphone again and spoke to the crowd about the importance of the Fourth of July, patriotism, and freedom. He gracefully looped and wove his story around so that he could speak about the tragedy that had befallen this small town. "I'm not telling you this story to make you sad," he said. "Today is a day of celebration and joy! I'm telling you this so that maybe you can find it in your hearts to make a donation at one of the two banks in this fine town, to take care of these young people and Jamie's family."

Then, with rebounding optimism, the announcer gave the names of each of the pony-tailed female contestants poised at the gates. One by one, they and their sturdy quarter horses thundered through the gates. Their expert, strong arms gracefully handled reins to finesse their steeds around two-toned steel barrels. Dust flew as they completed each of three tight loops.

One young woman lost her hat, and it not only left her head but became airborne from the speed at which she was travelling. Each rider rode like the wind, and then came to an abrupt halt, throwing on their equine brakes at just the perfect time. It was hard to tell who was happier, the horse or the rider, when they looked back and saw that their barrels remained upright, *and* the timer looked good.

The announcer, back in the swing of ribald fun and humor, and again, perhaps in defiance that life could ever be otherwise, made all his usual off-color and cringeworthy rodeo jokes. They were mostly about beer, beautiful women, and city slickers—often all three—and the crowd roared its appreciation and approval.

The crowd cheered on the competitors with encouragement and joy for the successes and gave sympathetic and somber moans for any failures. As the various rodeo events progressed—barrel racing, team roping, bronc and bull riding—the young men and women performed impossibly brave feats with barely domesticated animals, all wildly narrated by the salty old cowboy with the microphone.

People laughed and ate and drank, and they gazed out towards the surreal mountains all around.

As the rodeo finished, parents walked the tiniest cowboys and cowgirls back to the parking lot, to load up and head home. Those without young children trekked back downtown and found frivolity until the wee hours of the morning. Each of the town's three bars was full to capacity. The Silver Dollar Saloon was no exception. Surely the locals there made extra toasts to loved ones, to heroes, to Jamie. There were those thoughtful moments, but mostly it was a boisterous crowd in a bar known for its congeniality and warmth. It was a place where stories could be told and relationships fostered. That had not changed.

And for those hardy people anxious for the traditional last act of this holiday, they travelled over the pass to take in the fireworks in Virginia City. As those blissful colorful streaks filled up the night sky, friends held hands and proclaimed their gratitude for the gradual improvement of each of the survivors.

# Chapter 16

## *The July 5 Auction*

Following immediately on the heels of a very long July 3 and 4, many of Jamie's family members, the survivors and their families, and a crowd more than 300 strong turned out yet again on July 5. They gathered in the Ennis Lion's Club Park on this sunny Saturday evening. Susan Muchmore and her son and daughter-in-law, Chad and Cammie Sterzick, the owners of the Trading Post, put on an auction to benefit Jamie's family and all the survivors. These shop owners were the ones who were approached by a concerned tourist in their store, the day after the shooting. That woman gave them kind words, a donated flowerpot, and the seed of an idea for this event.

For Susan, Chad, and Cammie, the Fourth of July was one of their busiest days of the entire retail year. Usually they took a much-needed break on July 5. But this year, they rolled up their sleeves to host the biggest fundraising event Ennis had ever seen. They were assisted by Jan Coffman, whose daughter, Carrie, was the best friend of Kandi, Jamie's wife; along with Dulcie Clark, a local businesswoman and wife of Officer David Clark, the first Madison County Sheriff on the scene the night of the shooting.

Parking was scarce. Cars filled the parking lot and lined the street from the south end of town up to the business district, everyone eager for the auction, another barbecue, and a bake sale. The crowd nearly filled the sprawling Lion's Club Park. Families found shade among the cottonwoods, growing along the banks of the Madison River. While their parents paid attention to the auction, youngsters cast lines at the fishing pond. The pond was full of bottom-fed giant trout, which tasted terrible but kept the kids entertained.

The Madison Valley Women's Club had also joined in organizing the event. Women bearing beautifully crafted bake sale items streamed into the park. They set up a gorgeous display of their pies and treats and oversaw sales the entire evening. They donated their time and efforts despite being away from their families and houseguests.

The sizzle and scent of barbecuing burgers once again wafted through the warm evening air. The Ennis Lion's Club members, after providing a hamburger feast to the thousands the day before, now set up to provide yet another meal to many hundreds more.

At a small table inside the park's gazebo, a lovely red-haired woman sat with a stack of red and white bumper stickers in front of her. The words "LOVE WINS, Ennis, Montana" jumped out to any passerby. Her table would be empty by the end of the evening, every one of the hastily printed stickers having sold. That motto served as a rallying call, this small community's answer to an evil assault. The woman selling the bumper stickers was Kelly Kivlin, the best friend of Gavin Faulkner's mother, Maggi France. Kelly was the one who had danced with Gavin in Virginia City the night of the tragedy. These bumper stickers became the symbol of how the town of Ennis would direct all its energy, anger, passion, and hope into its future, and that of Jamie's family and of all the survivors. Proceeds from the bumper sticker sales were donated to those families.

The gazebo was the center of the action, and as the auction began, Susan took the microphone. The tall, dark-haired woman spoke with strong determination, "I want to welcome each and every one of you that came here today. I welcome all the out-of-town visitors, and most especially, I welcome each of the families here today that we have come to support and honor." With that, she asked Jamie Roberts' family to stand. "We are blessed to have with us today, Doug and Sharon Clark; Katy, their daughter and Jamie's sister; Kandi Popp, Jamie's wife and Kyra, Jamie's daughter." The family took a step closer to each other, as the warmth of the crowd enveloped them.

"I also want to welcome Ginger Powers, and her son, Cameron, and her whole family, Marilyn and Jim Powers and their other family members!" The crowd looked toward Ginger in her wheelchair. Her son, Cameron, elicited immediate laughter when he ran in the exact opposite direction towards the playground.

Susan also mentioned Matthew and pointed out a few members of the Ortega family who were present, along with Jaime and John Roberts who attended, representing Isaiah Crowley. Then she found Gavin Faulkner and Trett Sutter and their families and introduced them to the crowd as well. The introductions complete, Susan left the stage, turned the microphone over to a local photographer and flutist, Ken Hall. He officially opened the event with a poem and beautifully performed spiritual music to welcome all the attendees and to give some comfort to the families.

149

Once again, the community got some practice shifting from a moment of grief and spiritual care to a completely different energy. An auction! The volunteer auctioneers, Dan Reinoehl, Wayne Lower, and Mick Jackson, got on stage and started the bidding with great aplomb. They did their usual extraordinary job of keeping the auction and the bidding fun, productive, and moving right along. Other members of the community helped with registering bidders, organizing the massive number of donated items, recognizing bids, and collecting money from the far-flung, standing-room-only crowd.

More than 200 items were donated for the auction, and even after the event began, people were still bringing in more donations. Larry Zabel donated an original painting titled *The Meadows at Sterling*—a true visual representation of peace and tranquility. Larry was a highly esteemed artist in the valley who had been donating to causes for all the decades he had lived there. T. R. and Sandra Lane of Ennis purchased the painting for $10,000. No one missed the contrast between the peaceful scene in the painting and the events that led to this auction. They also did not miss the immensely generous and high price paid by the Lanes.

Ted Long, a highly accomplished local artist, donated an original pen-and-ink. Other artists provided beautiful pottery. An outfitter donated a four-day antelope hunt in Wyoming. A trip to Cancún, Mexico was auctioned along with a one-week stay in a condo during the cold Montana month of January. Three loads of gravel mix were sold from a local ranch, along with free delivery in Madison County. Local businesses donated countless gift certificates; craftspeople donated log furniture, jewelry, and other handmade items; and ranchers donated cut and wrapped locally grown lamb. Whatever people had, they gave. Then there were the t-shirts, baked goods, and dinner itself. All the proceeds went to the families.

The generosity, in both the donations and bids, was stunning. Then something even more remarkable began to happen. It started with Susan Snyder, a McAllister woman, who made and donated a beautiful handmade quilt with Jamie's and each survivor's name stitched on it. She titled the quilt "Broken Star." After she donated the quilt, she joined in on the bidding. To everyone's surprise, the quilt-maker herself kept bidding on the quilt until it reached the price of $6,500. At that point, Susan won the bid and paid that amount for her own quilt. As she left the gazebo, quilt in her arms, she walked right up to Jamie Roberts' sister, Katy. She smiled as she placed the quilt into Katy's arms.

Decades later, this quilt would still be among Katy's most prized possessions.

This bid-and-regift strategy was done more than once during the auction. A handmade Raggedy Ann doll made by Barbara Smith was put up for auction. Other people in the crowd got in a bidding war with Jay Willett, the Ennis High School Principal.

"And what will be bid now for this very fine handmade Raggedy Ann doll?" asked the auctioneer, looking directly at Jay.

"I bid $700!" Jay declared. Having leapt ahead in the bidding by $200, the other bidders quieted, and Jay beamed. He went to the gazebo and paid for the doll. Then he took the doll and found Kyra Roberts standing with her grandmother. He smiled kindly and handed the doll to Kyra, whose pretty eyes sparkled with disbelief and joy.

An Ennis second-grader, Courtney Dietz, who was friends with Mike Carroll's and Ginger Powers' son, Cameron, purchased two handmade Native American storybook dolls, only to turn around and gift them to her best friend, Cam.

Local sculptor Jim Dolan, perhaps best known for his life-sized herd of wild mustangs standing along Highway 287 on the way up to Helena, and whose hunter, horse, and grizzly sculpture graces the park in front of the Madison Valley Bank, donated an original sculpture for the auction. It sold at a very high price, knowingly bid high by the purchaser.

At the end of the evening, nearly $60,000 was raised.

Sharon Clark, Jamie Roberts' mother, climbed the steps to the podium and took the microphone. "I can't believe how wonderful this has all been, and I want to thank every one of you for coming here today and showing us so much love," she said tearfully. "I want to thank all the donors, all the bidders, with my heartfelt gratitude and appreciation."

Susan Muchmore joined Sharon and once more thanked everyone for their attendance. As the evening summer sun dropped lower on the horizon, the people mingled and slowly began to drift away to their homes, hotels, or tents and campers. Having witnessed so much loving, human kindness, they took a very special glow home with them.

# Chapter 17

## *More Donations Roll In*

The Ennis City Hall was, again, ablaze with activity. As of July 16, nearly $100,000, including the $60,000 from the auction, had been raised for Jamie's family and the survivors, to help defray funeral, medical, and living expenses. Ralph Hernandez, the Ennis Mayor, told a *Madisonian* reporter, "Within two weeks of the shooting, about $15,000 had been donated. At that time, a $2,000 distribution was given to each survivor, as was the family of Jamie Roberts. They were to use it however they wished."

Mayor Hernandez had been organizing the funds and appointed each member of the city council to a board to oversee their dispersal. "I wanted to make sure everything was kept public, so people could see where their money that they donated, was going," he said. "Except for the private trust in Kyra Roberts' name at First Madison Valley Bank, the board is in charge of everything, and it is all public knowledge."

The city council and Mayor Hernandez worked towards maximizing the benefit for everyone. All the shooting survivors had also received money from the Crime Victim's Compensation Fund to help defray medical expenses. This was monitored and applied for, on their behalf, by the Madison County Victim Advocate, Amy Cooksey. The Ennis Town Council Board also worked with Amy to make sure that local donations did not jeopardize funding from the state and federal level.

"We wanted to make sure they have enough to keep them going for now," Mayor Hernandez said. "All work being done on the victim's fund is volunteer, there are no administrative costs being taken from the funds. It is all going to the victims."

In the ensuing weeks, every checkout stand at Madison Foods, owned by Chris Gentry, had a jar with colorful lettering, explaining that donations would go directly to the Survivor's Fund. Many other businesses throughout town followed suit. As summer tourists made purchases at stores and shops, each clerk developed their own special heartfelt narrative to describe what this fundraising was for. Day after day, hour after hour, they shared their own abbreviated version of the tragedy and how much they wanted to help their friends. Store clerks and shop owners alike mentioned how telling the story over and over was hard, but it helped them heal too. It helped them find the words for something that still left them feeling choked up. The tourists responded with compassion and generosity. They donated with thoughtful acknowledgement of the pain this community was in; they were eager to give back to the people and the place that they loved so much.

# ~ ARTIFACTS ~

*A Community Cares for its Own*

# Letter to the Editor: Thank-You Card

## Section Barbara Smith, *The Madisonian;* July 16, 2003

To the People of Madison County, Ennis, Montana:

Once again you have shown to the world what true Montanans are. You've bonded together for the people in need in your small town. I want to thank you all, you make me proud.

I received a call about the doll that you auctioned at your recent benefit. I donated it hoping it would maybe go for $40-$50.00.

They called me and told me it was given to Jamie's little girl. That was so great! So I was told the story of the doll. It went for $700-$725 for one small doll. I will make another doll or two if you would like. Just let Linda Shipman know.

I know what the love of your small town means because I used to live in Ennis years ago. You were the same then too.

Love,

Barbara Smith

## Letter to the Editor: Thank-You Card Section
Clark Family, *The Madisonian; July 16, 2003*

We would like to express our sincere appreciation and thank you's to all who helped make it possible to get Jamie's trailer moved. We would like to especially thank Kenny Shirley and Mike Sprout for removing the skirting from the trailer, Gordy Matson (Matson Excavation), Cory Johnson, Brad Oldham, Tim Hoe (Hoe Construction), Laramie Houska, Mark Wolter, Dwayne Roedel, Don Pruetter, Lennis Crane for having his crane available, and Don Schaufler for pulling the trailer. We couldn't have done it without all of your help. We are truly blessed to have such good friends. God bless you all and thank you again for taking the time from your busy schedules to help us.

Thank you all very much,
Doug, Sharon & Katy Clark

~

## Letter to the Editor: Thank-You Card Section
Clark Family, *The Madisonian; July 16, 2003*

We would like to express our sincere thanks to the following people for making our dreams of having a flagpole possible. We would like to thank Susie Baldwin for giving her flagpole to us, Mike & Cindy McKitrick for sending Kenny Shirley and Spencer Noack to move the flagpole from Susie Baldwin's yard into ours. Again, thank you from the bottom of our hearts. You have all truly made us so very happy and proud to live in Ennis and the beautiful Madison Valley.

Thank you all very much,
Doug, Sharon & Katy Clark

# Chapter 18

## *Ginger and Mike are Home*

J ust a month after that terrible night, Joan Goetze, RN, parked her car outside the home of two much-beloved patients of Madison Valley Hospital. She and fellow nurses had arranged to make daily house calls to check on Mike Carroll and Ginger Powers. These house calls made it possible for the two to continue their recovery in the comfort of their own home, with their young son and other family members always close at hand. Marilyn Powers, Ginger's mother, let Joan in. The nurse and "the kids" all sat in the living room to chat. *The kids.* Joan had known Ginger and Mike their whole lives. But they were hardly kids anymore. This month alone, they'd shouldered enough hardship to last most people a lifetime.

"So, tell me how you both are feeling today," asked Joan.

"What I'm feeling is glad I don't have to go to the hospital this morning," Mike answered wryly.

"Well, it's certainly easier for one of us to come to you, than for you two to come to us!" Joan said, agreeing with his assessment of the situation. It was so good for them to be home.

Joan unpacked her bag of medical supplies and equipment. She took Ginger's and Mike's vital signs in the quiet of their own home, with Cameron playing nearby, and Marilyn in the kitchen helping with the cooking and cleaning.

There was a knock on the door and then whoever knocked let themselves in. Suzanne Powers, Ginger's younger sister, strode in. She immediately announced: "Joan, I'm ready for my first lesson on how to change their dressings!" Ginger looked down and smiled. How amazing it was that her sister would be willing to do this for her and Mike.

Joan drew and carefully labelled blood from each of her patients. Then, with Suzanne shadowing her, she checked and changed the wound dressings. All along the way, she continued asking both patients how they were feeling and healing. So far, so good. At least as far as the physical wounds were concerned. All the nurses and techs involved in this improvised home care program were inherently involved in caring for the survivors' soul wounds too. The simple acts of showing up, being present, and checking in with them every day worked wonders to let Ginger and Mike know that they were not alone. Yes, they were beginning to heal, in all ways.

Registered Nurses Joan Goetze and Jaime Roberts, along with Laboratory Technician Melinda Tichenor, took turns making these daily visits to Mike and Ginger's home to track their vitals, chat with them, take blood samples when needed, and then transport the samples back to the hospital lab for processing.

The Madison Valley Hospital stated early on that it would provide this extra medical support to all of the survivors at no cost to them. Anything other than a speedy and full recovery was simply not acceptable to any of the medical providers, staff, or the hospital's Board of Directors. There is no doubt that this commitment and loving care hastened the healing of each one of the survivors.

Later on that afternoon, Ginger sat in a comfortable chair in her living room, with the front door open. She looked out through the screen door at the green grass and fully leafed-out trees. A gentle breeze picked up a lock of her auburn hair and cooled her face.

A car pulled up out front, the driver's side door swung open, and yet another caring person got out, carrying a covered dish of lovingly prepared food. Ginger's eyes welled up once again, so grateful for the generosity that everyone had extended to her family. As she heard the footsteps coming up the walk, she called out, "Come on in!" The delicious scent of apples and cinnamon wafted through the screen door.

Cameron came into the room, no doubt drawn out of his room by the aroma. "Oh yum!" he said in greeting to the woman at the door. Ginger's mother, Marilyn, rushed out of the kitchen to open the door and receive the glass baking dish. The two women smiled and exchanged greetings, but the giver of the apple crisp couldn't stay for long. The baker hurried off, and Marilyn carried the crisp back to the kitchen. It would serve as dessert after several dinners that week, most of which were also provided by generous friends and neighbors.

Ginger sat in the gentle breeze and listened to her son's five-year-old antics, as he tried to "help" his grandmother in the kitchen. She could hear Mike moving around in the back of the trailer too. It was good to hear him up and at it. How happy she was that they were both finally home. Not only were they home; all the survivors were home and with their families now. At that moment, she really did believe, with all her heart, that everything would be okay, that they would all come through this just fine. With all the love poured on them by their families and their community, there couldn't really be any other possible outcome.

# Chapter 19

## *All the Survivors are Recovering*

On July 16, 2003, Holly Schmeck (Barney), a reporter for *The Madisonian*, gave a much needed and hoped-for survivor update. The greater Madison Valley community had been holding its collective breath to hear more.

Gavin Faulkner had returned home the same day of the shooting, wearing a cast on his thigh, and was undergoing intensive physical therapy. "I will return to University of Montana in Missoula to begin my second year in a few weeks," Gavin said. "I am really looking forward to this next year!" He spoke with his usual broad smile and warm demeanor.

Matthew Ortega, who had suffered damage to his colon, spleen, and diaphragm, was philosophical in his conversation with the reporter. "I no longer take anything for granted, and I believe that all of us survivors would say the same thing," he told her. "I think this is a positive change to my attitude, and I am pretty sure I have a more serious and mature outlook on life."

Trett Sutter shared that he was fully recovered physically, but still trying to understand the "why" of the tragedy. "I have to admit I am still searching for something positive to find which came out of this experience," he said. "But I believe I am doing well with that and moving forward in a good direction with my life." Like Gavin, Trett was staying focused on the future. He was planning to head back to school at Montana State University in Bozeman and "looking forward to a great second year of college education."

Isaiah Crowley told Holly, "I spent three days in the ICU at St. Vincent's in Billings. I still have one remaining bullet in my hip, of the four I took that morning. I will stay with Jaime and Shorty Roberts for three to four more weeks, and then continue my rehabilitation while staying with my dad in Missoula." He was doing physical therapy for his wrist, arm, back, and hip, hoping to regain full mobility so he could resume his career in construction.

Isaiah also shared how grateful he was that he had been able attend Jamie Roberts' funeral. The two had been close friends. He grew reflective and added that he was "working hard to fill my life with positive people and feelings and continue my focus on getting back to my full strength and physical abilities."

Holly couldn't help but notice that all these young people were staying so focused on being positive, and even more touching to her, staying connected to one another.

Mike Carroll and Ginger Powers shared that their lives were "forever changed." Ginger elaborated: "My perspective has permanently changed; little things are more important, and to me the most astoundingly true conviction I now have is that community is so important." She said she had a new realization that Ennis was a wonderful place to live. Ginger also added, more playfully, "Mike and I are still planning on getting married, but we think it might be best to wait until we are both able to walk down the aisle without medical equipment trailing behind us!"

Ginger and Mike were now taking care of Cameron together, with help from a strong and ever-evolving network of family and friends. She believed that because of all this loving support, she was sure they would both have a full recovery.

Mike told the reporter that coming home was the happiest day of his life. "Since the shooting I am much more dedicated to my family," he said. "This event was an eye-opener for me. I am now aware that things can change without warning, and you have to make the most and best of every day."

Mike had come very close to dying after the shooting. He was flown from Bozeman to Seattle, where he had part of his pancreas removed along with his gall bladder and a section of his intestines. Surgeons also patched a tear in his vena cava (one of the biggest veins in the body) and one of his vertebrae.

One of the medical providers who tended to Mike in the early morning hours of June 14 had noticed that a piece of fabric was deeply imbedded in his abdominal wound. The medical team speculated that the fabric had created a seal to the tear in the vena cava. Later, after more information came out about that morning, it became clear that Jason Klaumann had applied pressure to Mike's wound with some type of fabric. It was likely that, without Jason's quick thinking and care, Mike might have bled to death at the scene.

"I am trying to stay positive about what will likely be an entire upcoming year of recovery," Mike said. "My heart is full of love for the town of Ennis. I know that I have a long road ahead of me, but with all the support of so many people, my spirits will remain high."

When questioned about his feelings towards George Davis, Mike answered, "When I think of what he did to me, it doesn't make me mad, but when I think about what he did to Ginger, I want to be the one who kills him." These would have been ordinary words from some people. But to those who knew Mike Carroll, with his gentle demeanor and his willingness to be of help to anyone, these were very strong words indeed. It was noteworthy that his anger wasn't regarding his own situation, but in loving protectivity towards Ginger.

# ~ ARTIFACTS ~

*A Community Cares for its Own*

# Special Notice

*The Madisonian*; August 7, 2003

## FILL THE BOOT OF CARE
## BLUE MOON BENEFIT DANCE

**"Ennis Shooting Victims"**
**STEVE FULLMER & The Phantom Band**

**August 9**th
9PM
Cameron, Montana

$5.00 Cover Charge for Victims Fund

A COMMUNITY THAT CARES
Door Prizes * Door Prizes * Door Prizes * Door Prizes

**Letter to the Editor: Thank-you Card Section**
*The Madisonian;* August 7, 2003

It is hard to believe five weeks have passed this fast. The truly amazing thing is how fast our community came together to support everyone victimized by such a horrible act as the recent shooting of June 14th. Words cannot put into perspective the appreciation and thanks due to this community. We would however like to try to say thanks for all of the help we have been given. From moral support, to having auctions, fundraisers and donations to help all of us. It means a great deal to us and everyone else involved in the shooting.

Thank you.

Isaiah Crowley

John and Jaime Roberts

~

**Letter to the Editor: Thank-you Card Section**
*The Madisonian;* August 14, 2003

Thank you to everyone that contributed money and organized the fundraisers on our behalf.

Doug and Sharon Clark, Kandi Popp, Ginger Powers, Mike Carroll, Matt Ortega, Isaiah Crowley, Trett Sutter, Gavin Faulkner

# Chapter 20

## How Can He Plead Not Guilty?

*ugust 18, 2003* – Full of Madison County residents, the old frontier courtroom in Virginia City was hot and still, in the way it always is when August comes to Montana. Press stations were set up on both sides of the courtroom, with large camera equipment recording this momentous legal moment. The windows had been thrown open, but no breeze blew through to cool tempers and disappointments. Nearly every survivor was there, supported by loving family and friends.

Jamie Roberts' parents, sister, and wife sat in a tight knot along with Amy Cooksey for this hearing. Amy had prepared them as best she could for the expected "not guilty" pleas. The attorneys and the prosecutor knew that there would be no admission of guilt at this hearing.

When summoned by Fifth Judicial District Judge Loren Tucker, George Harold Davis stood, wearing his bulletproof vest. He was supported by his two capable court-appointed attorneys who flanked him tightly at the defendant's side of the front table.

Judge Loren Tucker read off each of the charges, one by one. "George Harold Davis, how do you plead to the charge of the deliberate homicide of Jamie Roberts?"

Davis wavered between his attorneys and did not raise his head.

"Not guilty," he muttered.

"How do you plead to the charge of attempted deliberate homicide of Mike Carroll?"

"Not guilty."

"How do you plead to the charge of attempted deliberate homicide of Ginger Powers?"

"Not guilty," Davis said and shuffled his feet.

There was some movement among the people in the gallery. Little could be done to truly ready them to hear this man deny the charges. Nothing Roberta Zenker nor Amy could have done could prevent how hard it hit them all, how thoroughly emotionally blasted they felt. There could have been no forewarning of how Davis's exculpatory words would physically feel to the victim's family and the survivors and their families. They were all still raw with grief, loss, rehabilitation, and gradual healing.

"How do you plead to the charge of attempted deliberate homicide of Isaiah Crowley?"

"Not guilty."

The heat became palpable. Bodies tensed. Feet fidgeted. There was a charge in the courtroom, but utter silence. Now, only the soft keying of the court reporter filled the silence between each plea.

"How do you plead to the charge of attempted deliberate homicide of Matthew Ortega?"

"Not guilty."

"How do you plead to the charge of attempted deliberate homicide of Gavin Faulkner?"

"Not guilty."

"How do you plead to the charge of attempted deliberate homicide of Trett Sutter?"

"Not guilty."

"How do you plead to the three charges of assault with a deadly weapon against Jake Stewart, Angela Hoe, and Nicole Toppel?"

"Not guilty."

The mood in the courtroom became thick and dank with rage and utter contempt. Amy had explained to Jamie's family that this hearing would be followed by a full trial regarding each of the charges. To some degree, the "not guilty" pleas meant nothing. But they also meant everything. Many harbored at least a residual hope that something human would emerge in the man, and he would accept blame for what he had done. It could have happened, but it did not.

George Davis had denied his accountability. Even though the process had been explained to them, the people could not believe that a person could have done this. There was complete silence. At the end of the brief arraignment hearing, two broad-shouldered Madison County sheriffs approached the defendant's table and ushered George Davis out of the courtroom, trailed by his attorneys.

After he and his attorneys left, people began to stir. As hearts began to beat again, and people found their legs, they rose and then held onto each other. The gallery slowly emptied. The only sound was the creaking of old wooden benches and footfalls. People gave each other awkward but warm hugs over the backs of these benches and in the aisles. Eyes met, many filled with tears. Everyone in attendance desperately tried to reach across the void, across the heartlessness of the day's legal proceedings.

# Chapter 21

## *If Looks Could Kill*

**If Looks Could Kill: The State of Montana vs. George Harold Davis**

Holly Schmeck

*First printed in The Madisonian; August 21, 2003*

On Monday, August 18, George Harold Davis lumbered into a silent courtroom teeming with emotion for his arraignment.

Davis is facing ten felonies stemming from the June 14 shooting of seven people in Ennis. Handcuffed and wearing a bulletproof vest, Davis sat in between his lawyers during the twenty-minute hearing.

About sixty people, most of them present during the shooting, attended the hearing. District Judge Loren Tucker had previously explained the charges to Davis during his initial appearance, which was held via a video conference, because Davis was still recovering from a gunshot wound, in Missoula.

One by one, Davis pled not guilty to one count of Deliberate Homicide, six counts of Attempted Deliberate Homicide and three counts of Assault with a Deadly Weapon.

Although facing a maximum penalty of death, County Attorney Roberta Zenker and John Connor, the DOJ Prosecution Services

Bureau Chief in Helena, will not make the decision to seek the death penalty until later in the trial process.

The defense had no objection to Davis still having no bond. They did request the right to hire a mitigation specialist[1] and a private investigator.

The prosecution team of Zenker and Connor had prepared their omnibus order[2], which outlined the expected motions to be filed by the prosecution and how long they expect the trial to take. The defense team, consisting of Ed Sheehy and J. Mayo Ashley, will also prepare an omnibus order as soon as they have all of the discovery material from Connor.

Based on the omnibus order, a schedule will be set for the trial. If Davis does not waive his right to a speedy trial, then the trial will be held within a year.

After the hearing, Davis was remanded to custody at an undisclosed location, not in Virginia City.

**Endnotes:**

[1]A *mitigation specialist* is an expert at finding legal reasons and rationale to impose a lesser sentence.

[2]The *omnibus orders* and hearing in a criminal matter outline the physical evidence and testimony that the prosecution has against the defendant and the expected pretrial motions and hearings that could arise based on that evidence.

# ~ ARTIFACTS ~

*A Community Perseveres*

# Fall and Winter of 2003/2004

*Time carried on. The seasons changed. The kids went back to school. But the Madison Valley did not forget Jamie's family and the survivors. For the next several months, the deep cold of a typical Montana winter contrasted starkly with the loving warmth spread at events honoring everyone affected by the Ennis 2003 shooting.*

~

### Letter to the Editor: Thank-you Card Section
*The Madisonian;* September 11, 2003

Thank you, thank you, thank you so very much to all of you for absolutely everything that you have done and continue to do for us. Thank you so much for taking such good care of us. All of your friendship, love, prayers, support, food, cards and gifts mean more to us than we will ever be able to say or show. Thank you all again, and very much.

Yours truly,

Ginger, Mike & Cameron

**Special Notice**

*The Madisonian*; October 2, 2003

**Ennis Lion's Club Annual**
**HALLOWEEN CARNIVAL AND**
**BINGO NIGHT**
FRIDAY, OCTOBER 31ST
6:00 p.m. - 9:00 p.m.,

Ennis Elementary School
GAMES, FOOD, PRIZES

Grand Prizes will be 2 awesome bicycles donated by
Ennis True Value Hardware.

"Bingo proceeds to benefit Ennis shooting victims"

∾

## Special Notice
*The Madisonian;* October 16, 2003

The Ennis Community Children's School, a non-profit organization, will be hosting its annual gun raffle and auction at The Silver Dollar Bar in Ennis. ECCS will be giving away snacks and drinks at a table outside The Silver Dollar during The Hunter's Feed. Any donations will be welcome.

The sale of 50/50 tickets will start at 7:00 pm downtown and the live auction will start at 7:30 pm in the Silver Dollar.

This year's fundraiser will support the Victim's Fund, the DiAnn Hokanson Memorial, and the Ennis Community Children's School.

Auction items have all been donated by local merchants and businesses.

∽

## Special Notice
*The Madisonian*; December 11, 2003

**Victims' Fund 9-Ball**

**Remember what happened in the early morning hours of June 14th?** Those of us in Ennis and the surrounding communities will never forget!

On December 14th, which marks the 6-month anniversary of this tragic event, there will be a 9-ball tournament at The Blue Moon Saloon in Cameron at 1:00 p.m. There is a $40 entry fee with prizes for 1st, 2nd, and 3rd place finishers, as well as a live auction and door prizes. The proceeds of this event will go to the victim's fund.

So come out and enjoy some complimentary grub, play some pool, and support the victim's fund!

## Special Notice

*The Madisonian*; February 5, 2004

### COME ONE – COME ALL

In memory of Jamie Roberts, (SLIM), his family and friends will be holding a Memorial Snowmobile Ride in his honor and also in the honor of the survivors. It will be held on Saturday, February 7th, starting at 10:00 a.m. at the Pioneer Bar parking lot in Virginia City. We will ride to Crockett Lake via Chuck Clark's cabin for chili and reminiscing. Hope to see many of you there.

Family and Friends of

Jamie Roberts, "Slim"

# Chapter 22

## The Memorial Ride

In February 2004, Jamie Roberts' friends and family organized a snowmobile ride to honor his memory and to honor all the survivors. The day had barely dawned when Doug and Sharon Clark, their daughter-in-law, Kandi, their daughter Katy, and their granddaughter, Kyra travelled over the Virginia City pass from Ennis to the small town of Virginia City. They arrived early as planned, just before sunrise, and parked their trucks and trailers carrying snowmobiles outside the Pioneer Bar. They unloaded their snowmobiles and spoke lightly to each other, their words making clouds of white mist in the cold morning air. They hoped the day would go well.

Suddenly, bright lights made them look up. They almost couldn't believe their eyes at the length of the procession of headlights gleaming towards them from vehicles coming down the Virginia City Hill. "Oh Doug, look at how many people are coming!" Sharon said to her husband. The two began pointing out the trucks that they recognized. There was Jody Sprout, a nurse at Madison Valley Hospital, and Dan Reinoehl, one of the auctioneers at the July 5 fundraiser. Of course, Chuck Clark's rig was in the line; he was the owner of the cabin they were riding to. Then there were Rob and Brenda Arrotta,

Joe Dickinson, Richard Todd, Jason Bjorngaard, Jon Swanson, Gene Hanni, Shawn Christensen (the Fire Chief) and his wife, Corrina, George Algers, Cooper Taylor, and others.

"I can't believe there are so many!" Sharon said. "I hope we have enough chili!"

There was plenty of shoulder jostling and wide smiles as the hardy group breathed mist and enthusiasm on this frigid morning. Men and women, young and not so young, got coffee in the bar, already trading jokes and stories. Soon, each member of this familiar group climbed aboard and revved up long, shiny snowmobiles and got ready to travel a route familiar to them all; it was a beloved trail from Virginia City to Crockett Lake. Many had traveled this route before with Jamie.

About halfway into the circular route, they arrived at Chuck Clark's cabin. The long procession of snowmobiles pulled around in front of the beautiful log cabin, all nestled into the spruce- and sage-covered hillside. As the riders dismounted from their sleds, the light from inside the cabin and the smoke curling out of the chimney were a warm and welcoming sight.

They all kicked snow off their boots and threw open the heavy wood door, entering the cabin's warm interior for the perfect chili, a warm fire, and happy reminiscing. The cabin filled with the sound of beverage bottles popping open and wooden chairs and benches scuffing the floor, and then the cheerful chatter of storytelling began.

This was the same cabin to which Jamie brought Cooper Taylor when Cooper was in danger of suffering from frostbite. These walls held many such experiences. There were somber thoughts with cheerful toasts and countless loving memories, as the chili feast commenced.

Sharon Clark stood and opened her arms wide to welcome everyone: "I want to thank you all for coming today and for taking time out of your own lives to celebrate with us, the life of our Jamie. I know he is smiling down on this room full of his favorite people!"

Several people stood and told their special stories of Jamie. They seemed to be trying to determine who could come up with the most audacious and treacherous snowmobile anecdote! Tears were shed along with warm laughter.

As the group left the cabin, they each nourished their own personal memories of Jamie, and said another farewell to him in their hearts as they continued onward to Crockett Lake. Here they looped back around to return to Virginia City. Jamie Roberts, that "happy-go-lucky, die-hard snowmobiler, friend, son, husband and father, good citizen and employee," as he was so lovingly described by Reverend Jean Johnson, would never be forgotten.

# Chapter 23

## *One Year Later*

June 14, 2004 – The friends and family of Jamie Roberts gathered at the Silver Dollar Saloon on the one-year anniversary of the shooting. They laid a giant wreath of flowers on the steps into the bar. A cheer went up when Doug, Sharon, and Katy arrived, and the celebrants nearest the door bustled them in, hugged them warmly, and passed them on to the waiting arms of others.

On this day these people looked upon one another and realized they were all survivors. They had so much love for each other, and nothing would ever change that between them.

This group also shared memories and food and drink, but mostly their conversation was directed towards the future. When they spoke of the past it was to share beautiful recollections. The tragedy was not forgotten, but the strong understanding and gratitude for what had survived in their town was paramount.

Outside the valley was green, and the sun was high and brilliant once more. Indoors, a group of healing souls shared their warm and fond memories of Jamie. Doug and Sharon Clark and their family were reminded once again that the town of Ennis would never forget Jamie, and these dear friends would hold them up whenever they needed a little extra support.

# Chapter 24

## *No Longer the Same*

**Memories of shooting linger: Ennis no longer the same since ranch hand killed one, wounded six a year ago**

Nick Gevock

First printed in The Bozeman Daily Chronicle; June 20, 2004
Excerpts from full article:

ENNIS – Teddy Lyon will show you the stool in the Silver Dollar Saloon where his friend Jamie Roberts always sat.

When he does, Lyon knocks on the bar, his way of saying hello to his friend.

Lyon babysat Roberts, who was killed a year ago in a shooting that shocked Ennis, and remained his friend through the years. But Lyon said he had never realized that Roberts had carved his name on the side of the wooden bar, right in front of his seat.

"Nobody ever noticed it," Lyon said this week, sitting on the next stool. "I was sitting here one day and looked down, and I went, 'Oh my God, he carved it in there before he died.'"

Roberts was a big strong man of 27 years who was beloved in the community. His persistent smile and good nature just made people want to be around him, Lyon said.

189

Ranch hand George Davis opened fire the morning of June 14, 2003, on a group of young people who were just coming out of the Silver Dollar Saloon, killing Roberts and wounding six others.

(EDITORIAL NOTE to PUBLISHER: Section break required; some text from original article omitted here, to avoid plot spoiler.)

A shooting so horrific would be stunning even in a large city. But it was devastating in this close-knit community of 840 people.

"I don't think the emotional scars will go away," said Heather Bourgeois, who works at the Ennis Trading Post, just a few doors down from the Silver Dollar Saloon.

Friends of Roberts gathered at the Silver Dollar Saloon this week on the one-year anniversary of the shooting to remember him. A wreath of flowers was placed on the outside steps of the bar, and his grave was decorated with a dozen wreaths and a sign reading "Class of '94, In Loving Memory."

Tourists often ask about the shooting, said Cami Sterzick, who owns the Ennis Trading Post. The tragedy made national headlines and people still remember.

But even worse is the effect the shootings had on residents' attitudes, Lyon said. People can't avoid checking out a stranger in a bar.

"It used to be that you would look at somebody and say 'Hey, how are you doing,'" he said. "Now you look at them and judge them."

Those suspicions have changed how seriously people take it when someone gets unruly in a bar, town police officer Tom Tighe said.

"If one customer gets kicked out of a bar, they usually call to the other bars to let them know there's a problem," Tighe said. "It was a pretty big eye-opener for people in the town that it could really happen anywhere."

But the people who were wounded are moving on with their lives. They're all back at work, although some of them had to make career changes because of their injuries and a few have moved away from Ennis.

The shooting has also helped reinforce the small-town values that bring people to Ennis, said Ginger Powers, one of the shooting victims.

"We're all a lot closer and more respectful of everybody," she said.

# Chapter 25

## *The Plea*

**A**ugust 27, 2004 – Amy Cooksey slowly drives up to the courthouse in her small compact car. It's 8:00 a.m. Friday morning, the sun has been up for about two hours, and it's already warm out. The old 1875 building glows in the rosy light. This is the oldest courthouse in Montana, a fact of which Amy is proud. She turns right, up the steep dirt road alongside the stately old courthouse building and parks just in front of St. Paul's Episcopal Church. She knows parking will be at a premium today and wants to leave the closer parking spots for those who are less able-bodied.

Amy rechecks the workbag on her passenger seat, noticing the newest statements at the front of her overstuffed case file, then she launches herself out of her car, full of energy to begin this momentous day. She is a tall, lean woman, and her long strides are purposeful. The case file she carries is a precious thing. Amy barely slept last night, and yet like many previous days, she is fully awake and ready. Today is the culmination of much of her entire past year's work as the Victim Advocate of Madison County.

She opens the back door of the courthouse and enters her miniscule office to the left of the rear door. Her hip bumps hard against the desk edge positioned too close to the filing cabinet, which is itself too close to the office door. She chuckles at her clumsiness. Maybe she is just a little nervous. As she sits at her desk, she settles herself and breathes deeply, steadying her thoughts.

So far, all is quiet in the courthouse. Amy has arrived an hour early to focus and review the statements entrusted to her to read aloud in court—from one survivor and two members of Jamie Roberts' family who aren't able to appear in person. She hardly needs to re-read them, but doing so calms her. Every word is emblazoned on her soul and in her memory. She spreads her notes across her desk and envisions once more how these three statements will weave in with those shared in person. She has worked closely with all the survivors and family members, and she's chosen a strategic order for presenting these survivor statements, one of which she believes will be the most cohesive and powerful.

She and County Attorney Roberta Zenker met all day yesterday. They have been working on nothing but this case for the past several weeks, and it has been their priority for the past year. In their meeting yesterday, Roberta shared with Amy that she was going to be rather bold during her closing statement, and she entrusted that plan to Amy. Their respect for each other has only deepened in the past year, and Amy told Roberta that she heartily approved.

Roberta and Amy also discussed the details of the final plea agreement between Davis's counsel and Roberta, as the attorney for the State of Montana, along with John Connor, from the Department of Justice. Amy already knew the key points. She knew that Davis would plead guilty to one count of homicide, and six counts of attempted homicide, and in exchange, the prosecution would drop their request for the death penalty.

After her final preparatory meeting with Roberta, Amy also spoke with Doug and Sharon Clark one more time. They let Amy know that Katy, their daughter—Jamie's sister—would come with them to court today. Now, Friday morning, as Amy prepares in her office, she can barely imagine what the three must feel this morning, on their drive from Ennis over the Virginia City Hill. What a beautiful mountain drive, what an immensely heavy day. Whatever Amy is feeling at this moment must be relegated to the back seat, so she can take care of the Clarks and all the others attending the hearing.

She is so ready to see them, these people who have become her very dear friends. She has spent so much time with them, shared so many conversations, both painful and healing. Amy is pretty sure she has connected on some significant level with every individual closely affected by the shooting. Along the way, she has maintained a meticulous log of her conversations with each one of these precious souls.

Whether they can attend in person today or not, Amy has done the best she possibly can to make sure that all of them understand what will happen. She has explained that the plea agreement is *not binding* on the judge, who may still throw it out entirely and set a sentence according to the sentencing guidelines of the state. But the agreement *does bind* the defense counsel and the defendant, as well as the office Amy works with, the Office of the Prosecutor of the Fifth Judicial District. Once Davis pleads guilty, that plea cannot be reversed.

Amy rocks back in her chair. She hears muffled voices and footsteps outside her door. People are starting to arrive. She takes a moment to reflect on something that has been nagging at her the past few days. She knows she has not kept her personal feelings separate from her job. She knows that about herself in general and certainly with this case specifically. Over the years she has been cautioned by professionals in her field to "not become emotionally involved," to "have a thick skin," and "keep it separate." All of that standard advice. But she has come to terms with the reality that, for her, that is simply impossible. Amy is in the prime of her life and career, and she comforts herself with her own personal conclusion: *she can handle it.*

She hears the back door open again and again, as courthouse personnel arrive. Usually, Fridays are quiet here. The presiding Circuit Court Judge of the Fifth Judicial District Court, Loren Tucker, normally holds court on Mondays in Virginia City. But this propitious matter has been set for Friday, the judge's "in chamber" day. Amy also hears and recognizes the voices of various law enforcement officers. They are setting up security checkpoints at the rear and front entrances of the courthouse. She isn't surprised. Amy witnessed similar proceedings one year ago for George Davis's arraignment hearing. The press will arrive soon, and with them, some curious onlookers. No doubt, tensions will run high.

Finally, a little before 8:30 a.m., Amy gathers her thoughts and her files and heads up the back staircase to the Fifth Judicial District Court of Madison County. The courtroom is up on the second floor. Upon entering, she saves several seats, placing some of her personal items along the first two benches in the gallery; she wants to gather all the survivors as close to her as she can. She greets the Clerk of Court and then the Court Reporter, who has driven 70 miles from Dillon and is now setting up to transcribe this event into this state's permanent legal records.

Amy wanders out through a side doorway, then through the waiting area at the top of the curving front entry stairs. It is approaching 9:00 a.m. She heads out onto a balcony at the front of the courthouse and watches the arrival of a steady procession of cars and trucks—everyone coming over the mountain pass from Ennis. They are parking now, up and down Wallace Street and all the streets surrounding the courthouse. People get out of their vehicles in twos and threes. They are thoughtfully dressed, and many lock arms or hands with one another as they join the silent tide filing up the grand stone steps outside.

The crowd backs up for a while, because of the weapons screening station that everyone must pass through. The ornately carved double doors are held open by the press of the crowd. Still, everyone proceeds through calmly. The officers speak personally to the people whom they know—which is almost everyone.

The first few people in the crowd are checked through, and Amy leaves the balcony to peer downstairs, watching them approach the grand curving staircase. They rest their hands on the polished wooden banister, the elaborately carved newel posts, and they begin their climb up the stairs to the courtroom. Amy hastily heads back to her saved seats, wanting to create a welcoming physical space for "her people" as they begin to arrive.

Another attorney has entered the courtroom through the back door. Karen McMullin has several cases before Judge Tucker this morning; her cases will begin after the criminal calendar has been cleared. She knew this momentous matter preceded hers, and she decided to attend. She has been following this case closely. As the only practicing attorney in Ennis, Karen has met with several of the survivors and their family members, advising them on ancillary legal matters and personal questions over the past year. She knows most of the young people well; her own four children were classmates of the survivors. She takes a seat in the far rear, for both a good vantage point and to make space for all those here with their hearts in their throats.

The imposing double doors at the top of the stairs are propped open. The people entering the gallery are silent. They take their seats on the red velvet-upholstered benches in the first row and on plain wooden benches throughout the rest of the gallery. Many mutely greet Karen with raised hands, nods, and solemn faces. They look to each other too, with similar silent greetings, everyone seeking out some measure of support and anchoring on this day when their senses are utterly raw. Many glance high up the wall at the framed black-and-white photos of fierce pioneer judges in Victorian garb. The portraits are at least familiar, if not particularly comforting.

Doug, Sharon, and Katy Clark enter, and Karen notices how Amy is watching for this family as well. Amy gestures for them to sit immediately next to her and hugs each of them. Mike Carroll enters, and there is a noticeable murmur of gratitude from everyone already in the gallery: he is walking—tall, proud, and sturdy. Mike also sees Karen and nods at her, and then he is immediately enveloped by the Clark family and Amy. Soon after, the family of Matthew Ortega enters. Others arrive, and the group of survivors and families forms and grows in the center front of the courtroom gallery, with Amy in the middle—standing, greeting, gesturing, hugging, and serving as a magnet to pull them all closely together.

Several other community members enter the courtroom wearing blue and red t-shirts bearing the initials JR, for Jamie Roberts. Under the initials is printed: *Just Remember, June 14, 2003.* The Clarks look up to quietly greet each of these supportive friends. Many approach the family, rest hands on their shoulders, and lean down to whisper words of support.

On this warm late-summer day, the windows behind the judge's bench and at the back of the gallery are wide open. The curtains on the windows are drawn back, and a gentle breeze sifts in, along with the sound of birds and a distant lawnmower. None of that brings any comfort or peace to the participants in today's proceedings. The air is fresh, but the atmosphere is heavy. People share a few more hushed greetings, and the wooden benches continue to squeak as the last few arrivals find seats. Then the double door on the left side of the courtroom flings open and everyone looks in that direction.

It's him. George Harold Davis shuffles in. Two serious-faced deputies hold his shackled arms and escort him, not too gently, to his seat between his attorneys on the left side of the council table. He wears a bulletproof vest on top of a garish orange jumpsuit. It is apparent that the deputies' task is twofold: to offer protection to their citizens and to protect this man from any boiling-over rage.

Davis's two court-appointed public defenders—Ed Sheehy Jr. of the Montana Office of the State Public Defender and J. Mayo Ashley, attorney-at-law—have their heads bowed over their files, and they politely greet their client. Mr. Sheehy whispers to Davis while Mr. Ashley reviews his notes.

These defense attorneys are seasoned at the role they play today. They are both well respected in the legal profession and know only too well how unpopular that role is. Both sit comfortably in this courtroom. Young and unseasoned attorneys might have felt the eyes from the gallery drilling into their backs. Not these gentlemen. For most of his career, Mr. Sheehy has led the office responsible for the criminal defense of the indigent and underprivileged in Montana. His co-counsel, Mr. Ashley, has practiced criminal law in Helena for decades.

Most attorneys have had the experience of representing a less than attractive or not-so-personable client. This is a far more complex occasion. These two men know that they are in this courtroom today, not only in furtherance of Davis's personal constitutional rights, but to preserve the time-honored legal system itself, under which every single person has a right to fair and unbiased judicial process. Both men seem well aware of the weight of that duty.

They both also know that this will be Davis's final courtroom appearance. At the end of this hearing, he will be sentenced. They have surely discussed how things may get out of hand during the survivors' statements, with all the emotion simmering in this gallery. It will be their responsibility to, as best they can, prevent that raw emotion from overly influencing Judge Tucker's sentencing decision. That is an onerous job, and these two men appear steeled to perform it.

The prosecuting attorneys are seated at the other end of the table: Roberta R. Zenker, Madison County Attorney, and her co-counsel, John Connor, from the Montana DOJ Bureau of Prosecution Services. These two look primed for battle with erect and attentive posture. They do not speak to each other; both look straight ahead, watching the entrance to the judge's chambers.

The courtroom is full, with a few standing in the corners at the back of the gallery. There are court officers and sheriffs, the local press, and citizens of the Town of Ennis and Madison Valley. This crowd has not seen Davis since his arraignment hearing. That was last year, but his "not guilty" pleas still ring in their ears.

The Clerk of Court, Bundy Bailey, stands and commands, "All rise!" There is a rush of air as everyone in the packed courtroom stands simultaneously. The Honorable Loren Tucker enters from the judge's chambers, and his black robe swings out behind his tall and elegant frame as he strides toward his podium. All is silent until Judge Tucker tells the packed courtroom to be seated. There is the squeak and rustle of clothing and bodies, then all heads look forward, expectant.

Karen knows that Judge Tucker is well known to everyone present in the courtroom. He followed Judge Frank Davis to the bench, and previously served as Madison County Attorney—with Roberta R. Zenker as his Deputy. Since becoming the Fifth Judicial District Judge, he has presided over many serious matters, including Davis's arraignment hearing the year before. Judge Tucker is known in the state for his regal bearing, his fairness, his surprising sense of humor, and his strange affection for obscure verbs and adjectives. Most importantly, he is known for his formality. He maintains tight control over the proceedings and people in his courtroom. Those who have only observed Judge Tucker's somewhat austere, dignified courtroom presence might be surprised to see him in another context: serving as a Lion's Club auctioneer of great skill and wit. There are many community members present who know that Judge Tucker is a man of contrasts.

He calls the proceedings to order and introduces the case. The judge inclines his head towards the Clerk of Court, who stands, and reads aloud: *The People of The State of Montana versus George Harold Davis, Cause Number DC-29-03-13 is before this Court.*

Then Judge Tucker begins: "I want to welcome the community members of the Town of Ennis and the Madison Valley to today's hearing, and particularly I want to welcome all the survivors and their family members whom I recognize and see in this courtroom today." Turning his attention to the defense counsel, the judge adds, "Gentlemen, I understand there is to be a Change of Plea in this matter today. Is that correct, Counsel?"

"That is correct, Your Honor," says Mr. Sheehy.

The judge asks Davis to stand. With his hands held tight in front of him and his lank brown hair falling into his face, Davis leans forward then stands. As he rises, so do his attorneys on either side of him.

Karen cannot help but look at this thin, unprepossessing man and struggle to connect his unremarkable appearance with his actions over a year ago. How could such an ineffectual-looking person have such an impact on her community?

Judge Tucker continues, "Mr. Davis, it is my understanding that your defense counsel and the attorneys for the State of Montana have reached a plea agreement. Is that correct?"

Davis looks bewildered, and his counsel, Mr. Sheehy, whispers into his ear. But Mr. Ashley jumps in, speaking for Davis, "That is correct, Your Honor."

The judge turns to the prosecution and asks them to confirm as well. "That is correct, Your Honor," says Ms. Zenker.

Then Mr. Sheehy stands and addresses the judge, summarizing the plea agreement:

"Your Honor, our client has determined that rather than stand trial in this community, he will plead guilty to these charges, in exchange for which the prosecution has dropped their request for the death penalty. These are the terms of the plea agreement entered into between the prosecution and the defense."

Judge Tucker looks at Davis and asks:

"Have your attorneys explained to you, Mr. Davis, that this court is under no obligation to accept this plea agreement, and that your change of plea today will not guarantee to you that I will implement any of the sentencing portions of the plea agreement entered into today between your defense counsel and the prosecutor of the state? That it will be within my discretion to sentence you as I see fit?"

Davis shuffles his feet and looks straight down at the desk. Mr. Sheehy leans toward his client, with his elbow grazing his side, and again whispers to him. Davis finally speaks for himself: "I understand, Your Honor."

The few reporters allowed inside the courtroom are recording every bit of this to transmit to their hungry readers all over the state and nation. There is one camera set up. The print journalists are all seated in one small area at the rear of the courtroom, furiously taking notes.

Judge Tucker nods at Davis and proceeds with what the entire courtroom is waiting for: the charges and formal pleas. "Very well then, George Harold Davis, you are charged with one count of Deliberate Homicide, for the murder of Jamie L. Roberts, as described in Section 45-5-102, Montana Code Annotated. How do you plead to that charge, sir?"

There is no sound, and then a sharp intake of breath by many people at the same time. All present remember the hearing in this very courtroom a year earlier—how inconceivable that this same man could stand there and utter the hateful words "not guilty" over and over in a drumbeat of hideous denial.

"Guilty, Your Honor," says Davis.

There is a collective exhalation by all those souls so bitterly relieved by that one word coming out of the mouth of this one particular man. Every single person in Amy's realm moves closer to each other. Her face shows the slightest release of tension and so do many others. This word, this admission, will never bring Jamie back. But this is now an accounting in the universe for his absence, amongst all these people who will always love and forever miss him. This moment is clearly crucial to their healing.

The judge waits and then says: "George Harold Davis, you are further charged with six counts of the Inchoate Offense of Attempted Murder described in Section 45-4-103, Montana Code Annotated. You are charged with the attempted murder of Michael Carroll. How do you plead, sir?"

"Guilty," says Davis.

"You are charged with the attempted murder of Matthew Ortega, how do you plead?"

"Guilty."

"You are charged with the attempted murder of Gavin Faulkner, how do you plead?"

"Guilty."

"You are charged with the attempted murder of Isaiah Crowley, how do you plead?"

"Guilty."

"You are charged with the attempted murder of Ginger Powers, how do you plead?"

"Guilty."

"You are charged with the attempted murder of Trett Sutter, how do you plead?"

"Guilty."

One after another, Davis pleads guilty. But his tone is flat. He slouches the whole time. There seems no remorse in this man's bearing. Rather than sincere, he merely seems beaten. Does that matter? He has admitted full guilt. All recognize the legal power of those words, sincere or not. The courtroom is silent. Everyone present feels the weight of this: *Davis has admitted full responsibility for his horrifying crimes.* Everyone present also cannot help but measure those admissions against the daily burdens and losses that they have borne for over a year.

The old wooden benches squeak as the family and friends of Jamie, the survivors, and their loved ones shift in their seats. They prepare themselves for their personal part in the proceedings. Judge Tucker knows the moment is full of energy needing outlet, and he takes firm control of his courtroom by stating to everyone present, what exactly will occur next:

"At this time, the people who have been impacted by the crimes to which the defendant has pled guilty today will have their time to be heard. It is this court's duty to honor and take into consideration those statements made here today in determining what the appropriate sentence will be for the defendant. I want to remind all the people who wish to speak, that this is a courtroom, and as such, its decorum must and shall be preserved, and all must comport themselves in a dignified and honorable manner."

Brows furrow and many hands tremble, as the speakers prepare themselves. They have all worked with Amy; they have their written speeches in hand. Amy looks around at this group and feels the great responsibility she has taken for them and for those who are not present today. But she is ready. She looks down at her own notes as they all wait to be called up.

Amy is sandwiched between Doug and Sharon Clark, and she alternately leans toward each of them. Unlike last summer's arraignment and omnibus hearing, this day is different. She thinks about how amazing it is that she and Ms. Zenker were able to garner a unanimous agreement amongst all the survivors, their families, and Jamie's family. They are all willing to forgo a full jury trial, which would have aimed at obtaining a unanimous guilty verdict and death sentence.

Jason Klaumann is not present today. He has been "standing by" for the entire year, continuing to work at his job in Salt Lake City, but always ready to come full speed to Virginia City if Amy requested it. She has been his communication lifeline, keeping him posted on all new developments in the case. Her constant updates truly made it possible for Jason to stay on at his job in Salt Lake. He was ready to serve as the State of Montana's star witness for the prosecution. But he too, affirmed the wisdom of the plea agreement.

Amy and Roberta worked for weeks explaining thoroughly what a full jury trial entailed, how painful it could be for crime survivors. All would need to testify and, following a lengthy trial, there could be years of appeals and further legal proceedings, again possibly requiring the survivors and their families to give testimony yet again. With the plea deal, the prosecution dropped the request of the death penalty, but Davis would admit full guilt. And the survivors would be done with their part in the legal proceedings. They could attempt, in whatever way they could, to move on.

But first, several of them have statements they want to share.

Amy is ready now to support her clients who are physically present: most of the six survivors and their families, along with Jamie's family. They have all been practicing with her, rehearsing some of the most momentous words they will ever speak about a trauma so scarring, so damaging, and still so raw, that few words exist to describe it. They will do so now, not only for themselves, but as an act of solidarity, holding and assisting each other today as a singular group bound by shared pain.

Amy can practically hear Doug's heart pounding. He will be the first to speak. Earlier that morning she shared a little dark-humor moment with him. "If you do pass out while speaking, I'll catch you," she said, "I promise I won't let your head hit the floor!" They both chuckled. Now all she can give him is her presence.

Doug stands and heads to the front of the courtroom, with Amy trailing closely behind. He enters the witness box next to the judge, and Amy perches on a stool nearby. He is not alone. The clerk asks

Doug to raise his hand and swear "to tell the truth." Then this slight man so beloved in his community, looks to the notes in his hand, and begins to speak.

"I walked out of the Silver Dollar bar just in time to hear gunshots, and as I looked towards the sound, I saw my son, Jamie Roberts, fall to the ground, and everything in my father's heart prepared me for the fact that my son could be mortally wounded." Doug takes a breath and faces the man who killed his son:

> "George Harold Davis, can you imagine what that was like for me? Then, in the next moment, I see my friend, Mike Carroll has also been shot and he is blown backwards into my arms, crying out 'My God I have been shot!' I hold Mike up, and pull him backwards into the bar, not knowing where you are or where the shots are coming from."

Doug looks away from Davis. He turns his attention to the judge and continues to describe what he went through:

> "I then gently put Mike into Nicole or Angie's arms, and ran to my son, and attempted to give him CPR. I felt that I may be too late, but I could not give up. I then was faced with the task of loading my son's seemingly lifeless body into the bed of my friend Scott's pickup truck and taking him to Madison Valley Hospital, with some small hope for a miracle."

One final time, Doug passionately addresses Davis, pointing his finger at him, and saying, "You will be judged by God! I will never forgive you for all the pain you caused to me, my family, and the entire Ennis community, and that because of what you did, I simply cannot find forgiveness for you in my heart."

Davis makes no eye contact with Doug. He only looks down. His hands are still. There are tears throughout the gallery. All are silent as Doug rises and, taking the step down from the stand, returns to his seat.

Amy remains seated on the small stool behind the witness stand. She will stay here for some time, a literal supportive presence. Sharon, Jamie's mother, rises to go to the witness box and swear in. Amy pats the woman's shoulders as she sits down in the witness chair, then Amy scoots back to her own stool. Sharon's usually gentle voice is transformed. Today she is an enraged mother, and all present feel her power. She begins with addressing Davis directly:

"I will never be the same person that I was since you, George Davis, shattered and tore one of the biggest holes in my heart, for which there is no repair as I desperately need my son Jamie here on this earth with me and not in Heaven with God. You took him out of the world faster than I brought him into this world!"

There is a pause as Sharon collects herself, and everyone in the courtroom absorbs her words. Then she continues:

"You not only took Jamie away from me, but you also left his father without a son, his sister without a brother, a wife without a husband and most important, his daughter Kyra without a daddy, and the rest of Jamie's family and friends without one of the most important persons in our lives. How do you explain to a four-year-old that some very terrible person took her daddy and shot and killed him? … I as his mother cannot understand why you acted out the way you did the night of June 14, 2003."

Sharon takes a moment to address the judge, describing the day her family was told about the plea agreement, back on March 29. "Finally this man became accountable… March 29th was Kyra Roberts', my granddaughter's, fourth birthday, and I will have to explain to her in the future that she got the best birthday present imaginable when George Harold Davis finally owned up to what he had done."

Sharon takes a breath and turns her attention back to Davis. She has reserved her most searing words for this moment:

"I feel that you also killed me that horrible night of June 14, 2003. You, George Davis, killed my one and only son. Jamie was one of the kindest, most outgoing, happy-go-lucky people anyone would want to be around. Jamie liked to make the whole world laugh and be happy. Jamie had no enemies.

"You deserve nothing more than to rot in hell! I will find it impossible to breathe the same air as you. As Jamie's mother, I want you to stay in a maximum-security prison for the rest of your life without any visitors, or the chance to breathe the fresh air outside or see the sun rise or set ever again."

Then Sharon, suddenly once more a gentle recognizable soul, stands from the witness box and heads back toward her seat in the gallery. As she approaches her family, she reaches for Doug's hand. The distance between them closes, she collapses to her seat, and they hold tightly to each other.

Now Amy herself stands and enters the witness box to be sworn in, to read the written testimony of two more Clark family members: Grandmother Beulah Clark and Kandi Popp, Jamie's widow. Amy speaks aloud a grandmother's fiery rage and the broken-hearted words of a young, bereaved wife. Three of the most salient sentences are Kandi's: "People say that time eases pain. I don't think that is true. It has just made us miss Jamie even more."

Amy returns to her stool behind the witness box and beckons Katy Clark. Amy has one more written survivor statement to share, but not yet. All of the Clark family will have their chance to express themselves first and then any other survivors who wish to speak in person.

Jamie's sister, Katy, leaves her family in the gallery and approaches the witness box. She is sworn in and looks to Amy for a moment. Then she, too, gives her own impassioned speech to Davis. Finally, she asks him: "Why?" She answers the damning question herself, pointing out that he has shown no remorse. She tells Davis that the only reason she can discern for why he did what he did is that he "is the devil!"

Judge Tucker listens to these raw, charged statements with his usual regal bearing and tendency towards the formal. He shifts uncomfortably at the constantly repeated phrase "burn in hell." It clearly discomfits his sense of propriety. Yet, not once does he directly caution a witness, nor constrain their obvious need to say those words. Although his expression suggests that he would like to stop such phrases from being used in his courtroom, he allows his fellow community members to vent their horror and grief.

Katy returns to her seat, and Mike Carroll approaches the witness box. Once more, gentle smiles fill the gallery—so many people thankful that Mike is walking once more. He raises his hand and is sworn in, then begins by reiterating that great question on everyone's mind: "Why?" Then he continues, addressing Davis directly: "I talked to you that night, yet you shot me and you shot Ginger. I condemn you most of all for shooting Ginger." Notably, Mike gives no further emphasis on all that he had to bear in terms of his own physical rehabilitation and long path to recovery. His rage at Davis is primarily focused on how much harm he caused Ginger. Mike finishes, stands, and returns to his seat.

Amy again stands from her seat, and the clerk allows that Amy is already sworn in and may take the witness stand. She does so and begins with stating that Matthew Ortega, who is living in Minnesota now, has also asked her to read a written statement. Amy addresses Davis on Matthew's behalf:

"What you, George Davis, did, was wrong, but I, Matthew, forgive you for what you did. I forgive you because I will not let someone, or a situation like this beat me or bring me down. I believe that in any situation you have only two choices, to stay down or to get back up. No matter how hard it is, you must try your very hardest to get back up."

Amy stands, and absolute quiet settles over the courtroom. She gathers her notes and makes her way to her cadre of survivors. No one speaks, but bodies shift to allow her back into the group. The wisdom and weight of Matthew's words reverberate throughout the room. The injury done to these people was grave. However, all but one are still here, and the survivors have come here as one. Matthew's words tie them all together; this community is still here, intact, and some have even entered a space in which they are able to forgive. People glance around looking for the Ortega family. Their eyes give gentle assent, affirming that a truly wondrous thing has just occurred. This boy, one of three gravely injured survivors, has shared a message of forgiveness, and the Ortegas should be very proud of their son.

No more survivors or family ask to speak. For a moment, the courtroom is silent. The community of survivors huddles in the stillness, breathing collectively, realizing they have completed their mission here today. One can almost see the web of support and collective understanding holding them together. There is no separateness amongst them. Some of the survivors present have suffered such a devastating loss that forgiveness is not possible; it may never be. The community that has supported them this past year knows this and embraces them, along with their enormous hurt and loss. Nothing more will ever be expected from them. And those who have reached a stage of forgiveness will be honored for that. There is enough love in the community of Ennis, Montana, to encompass the full range of emotions in every heart of every survivor.

Finally, Ms. Zenker stands. This is the moment that she was referring to when she alerted Amy of her plan to take a significant risk in her closing statement. Ms. Zenker has rarely been so invested in an outcome in her previous cases before Judge Tucker. She knows this judge well, and she knows that to provoke his ire could lead to an undesired outcome. She cannot risk doing so today, yet she feels with all her heart that she must impress upon him how she views this particular case, this particular defendant.

She wants to make certain that Davis will not *ever* have the possibility of being out of prison on parole. She knows with certainty how that would affect all these people with whom she has worked for the past year. Still, this is a substantial request of the judge: the denial of any future hope of parole.

She must somehow stay within Judge Tucker's limits, but she girds herself to make an emotionally charged closing argument. She will push against the boundaries of this judge's sense of decorum. She looks up at Judge Tucker, her former boss, whom she knows so well. Then she begins, "Your Honor, it is the State of Montana's position that George Harold Davis be sentenced to a life of confinement in a high-security prison…without ever there being a possibility of his parole!"

This is a highly unusual sentence for any criminal matter. Yet Ms. Zenker feels that should Davis ever get out of prison, the community will be immediately at risk. The only way they can have any peace is if there is zero possibility of his release.

The judge looks down, and everyone present tries to read that small gesture.

Ms. Zenker continues leading the judge down her philosophical path by asking the court, "Why did he do it?" She rushes in with her answer, "George Harold Davis is evil incarnate. He is the very face of evil."

That statement hangs in the air. Everyone in the gallery feels a resonant agreement; these words are the only possible answer to the imponderable questions they have harbored in their own hearts.

Ms. Zenker knows she may be dressed down by the judge, but she is emboldened by the weight of what this community has had to bear. She tells the judge, "Davis's background is full of violent tendencies. He is brutal, dangerous, and evil. He is a racist and white supremacist, and he has been quoted as saying that Hitler should have been successful!" Ms. Zenker reminds Judge Tucker that Davis once harassed an Idaho sheriff simply because his last name was Goldman. Davis advocated for paramilitary groups, served as a mercenary in Nicaragua, and had shopped for a sniper rifle.

Much of this information about Davis's past has already made it into regional news publications; Ms. Zenker knows this. But she feels a pressing need to knit it all together clearly. She wants to show Judge Tucker that Davis has a lifelong habit of never contributing to society in any positive manner. She believes there is no moral "balancing act" for the judge to consider when sentencing this man.

The people in the courtroom follow along with this intense description of a life horribly lived. There is no compassion, but there may be a universal understanding of how utterly wrong one human being can become. We are all granted one beautiful singular life, and somehow, some humans corrupt their entire time here.

Ms. Zenker pivots towards the gallery, although no one present thinks for a second that she is not still addressing the judge—who has gone very still. "Davis is a cancer, and the court is the surgeon! The community asks the court to remove this cancer from among us forever!"

No one stirs. The metaphor is impassioned and persuasive. Judge Tucker does not dress down Ms. Zenker for this inflammatory language. He simply listens. Her closing statement complete, Ms. Zenker returns to her seat.

Mr. Sheehy rises and requests permission to address the court. He then speaks to Judge Tucker, "Your Honor, the defense requests that you take into account the mitigating factor that George Davis had been taking the medication Paxil at the time of the crime." Mr. Sheehy goes on to explain that it is well known that alcohol and Paxil interact dangerously. Davis's significant alcohol consumption and medication doubtless influenced his behavior. Mr. Sheehy wants the judge to consider this factor in his sentencing. A similar defense has been used before, in a previous criminal trial in Gallatin County, Montana. It's known as "The Paxil Defense." It's paltry at best, but what else is there for someone guilty of such horrors?

The courtroom is quiet. The only sound is that of reporters scribbling away, the soft swish of the court reporter's keyboard. Judge Tucker, too, makes notes in his own notebook. There is a pause, and all feel a freight train of energy simultaneously.

Judge Tucker scans his notes, clearly taking time to mentally compose his next words. Finally, he looks up and speaks to the riveted courtroom, "I am unmoved by the defense counsel's attempt to rehabilitate George Harold Davis in the eyes of this court, and with your attempts to mitigate Davis's actions." The judge's blazing gaze is now solely upon the defendant, who has finally raised his head:

"You have shown no sympathy for any of these victims up until this very hearing. I do not buy the efforts of the defense counsel that I should be persuaded by the defendant's use of the drug, Paxil, and his voluntarily withdrawing from that drug. It was a result of the defendant's taking that drug combined with alcohol, which led to his outburst. It was Davis's own choice to drink ten beers that night! I feel the heartfelt anguish expressed by the victims of these crimes and the only fortunate point is that only one person was killed that night. Had George Davis been a better marksman, more people would have certainly died. It was not for lack of effort!"

The judge pauses, then looks out over the gallery and addresses the greater community, "I warn you all in this courtroom today to not expect much from my decision. We do not live in a perfect world. There will be no perfect result. That's the only thing that I can promise. The court must operate under the rule of law. What that is evil, and what that is good, that final judgment must be left to God!"

Now, Judge Tucker takes a deep breath, and so does everyone with him. He sentences George Harold Davis: "You, sir, are sentenced to life in prison, without the possibility of parole…the fact that you were so willing to take other people's lives leaves the court with little choice but to impose such a sentence."

He also sentences Davis to pay $76,000 in restitution to the victims. Amy had taken pains to explain to all the survivors that any restitution amount would be wholly inadequate, given their actual financial losses. It did not even begin to touch upon their collective medical expenses and lost wages. The restitution is a gesture only. They know that. Honestly, no one cares. In order for that sum to be of any consequence, it would necessitate Davis's release, his return to a workplace, and garnished wages as a condition of his probation. No one wants that. No one wants him out in society ever again.

The judge stands, and some scramble to rise with him as he turns and takes his stately leave into his chambers.

There is an outburst of crying, and simultaneously, some awkward clapping throughout the gallery. Most people turn toward someone. They all come together, with arms reaching out and over the backs of benches, some standing, some remaining seated. Among the survivors and their supportive friends, there is no one alone in this courtroom. Hands grasp shoulders and forearms. Many embrace each other in support and caring concern.

The two sheriff's deputies approach the conference table behind Davis and his attorneys. His attorneys stand and lightly clap him on the back, murmuring a few parting words. The officers set strong and diligent hands upon Davis's arms, as they take custody of him for what will be the remainder of his life. The gallery turns silent once more, as George Harold Davis leaves through the front exit and down the stairway to the left—the passageway to the Sheriff's Department and the holding cells.

The hearing is adjourned just before noon, and the Old West courtroom is, not for the first time, filled with the deepest human emotions that exist. Men don hats, women gather purses, and with heads bowed, the exodus begins.

Unsurprisingly, this moment affords no closure. There is no sure sense of finality. Each person leaving carries their own heartful of feelings. There cannot be relief until they each take their measure of one another. That unwieldy process begins as words and hugs are exchanged, and they take their first steps out of the courtroom.

An orderly procession ensues with no instruction needed. This mass of caring humanity moves in rapt cohesion with each other, having shared so much of their lives together.

Karen, having other matters before the court this day, stays. She meets eyes with Amy, in recognition. They know each other well, having handled appalling child abuse cases together over the years. Karen is impressed, as always, as Amy gently touches backs, guiding and guarding her people.

Amy leaves with them all, out through the double doors and down the beautiful, carpeted stairs. Outside, the stream of humanity continues down the courthouse steps, toward parked cars, up and down Wallace Street, and behind the old courthouse building. A crowd forms at the bottom of the steps with Amy and the Clarks in the middle. All around, the streets fill with talking, hugging, embracing, and weeping. Amy weaves amongst the survivors and their closest supporters. She makes sure she has contact information for each, because she is not done with these people. She will remain available to them, should they need her, and she imparts those words over and over again.

Community members embrace each survivor and the Clark family. There is talk of future get-togethers, memorials, shared meals. The connection forged amongst these people is not to be severed, ever. Doug and Sharon and several others happen to look up and out toward the street, just as a car passes by bearing a bumper sticker that reads:

LOVE WINS
Ennis, Montana

## Chapter 26

## *You're Never Over It:*
## *Recovery is a Continual Task*

Amy Cooksey was eating a sandwich on a park bench next to the Ennis Pharmacy on a summer day three years after the shooting. Mike Carroll approached her and sat down beside her. He connected with her with ease, updating her about his life. Within minutes, Gavin Faulkner strode across the lawn and joined them in the warm sunshine. Gavin too, caught Amy up with what was new in his life. The two young men knew each other well. It was clear to Amy that if they weren't close three years ago, what they survived together had forged a tight bond. She smiled to herself, appreciating this.

Amy was able to ask just the right caring questions to allow both young men to honestly speak about their lives and new challenges. They continued to connect with Amy over the years, grateful to have someone they could speak with openly about the difficult, long-term, ripple effects of surviving a violent attack.

Ten years after the shooting, in 2013, Gavin Faulkner's mother Maggi France, found and reached out to Amy, sharing that she believed her son was not doing well and needed some assistance with substance abuse. This was a full decade after Amy had forged a professional connection with her son. It had been years, but there seemed to be a connection between what Gavin survived in 2003 and his current struggles. Maggi knew that Amy genuinely cared for Gavin. She was sure Amy would help, and she did.

Amy used her resources, telephoned a number of contacts, and was able to obtain counseling for Gavin, even though he was then residing out of state. Gavin recalled, "I was living in Las Vegas, Nevada, and in the deepest, darkest thralls of my addictive years... Amy was quick to research and put my mom in touch with great counselors for me in Las Vegas, and I did follow up." He adds that, at that time, he wasn't able to quit. But the fact that people cared that much planted a seed. Within another five years, he enrolled in a program that helped him successfully get sober.

Today, Amy remains in contact with some of the survivors and the family of Jamie Roberts. She kept in touch even after she left the position of Victim Advocate for Madison County, Montana.

# Chapter 27

## *The Survivors, Twenty Years Later*

DOUG AND SHARON CLARK, parents of JAMIE ROBERTS, and FAMILY

Doug works for High Mountain Extremes Excavation Company in Ennis, Montana, but hopes to slow down in the future. His wife, Sharon, has enjoyed retirement for a year. Sharon and Doug still get extra meaningful hugs from people in town. They know in their hearts that those hugs are given in the hope of lessening the remaining burden of their loss and to confirm once again that, in this small Rocky Mountain town, "Love Wins."

Katy Clark, the sister of Jamie Roberts, is married to her high school sweetheart, Jaron Loucks. She works for a dental office in Three Forks, Montana.

Kandi Popp Roberts, Jamie Roberts' widow, is now married to Jay Swecker. Jay owns an auto body repair business in Billings, Montana, and Kandi keeps the books for the company.

Kyra Roberts, the daughter of Jamie Roberts, is now a young woman who has a lovely young son. She also resides in Billings.

❖ ❖ ❖

## MIKE CARROLL

Mike Carroll still lives in Ennis. Mike has all the youthful charm he was born with and continues to be a beloved member of the community. He is a most private man; and that wish of his is firmly honored, as is he.


## ISAIAH CROWLEY

Isaiah Crowley works as a superintendent for a construction company in Bozeman, Montana. He lives on the same street as Jim Deming, the psychologist who worked at the grief counseling session held in Ennis, just days after the shooting. He has been with Cara for seventeen years, and they are planning to move to Arkansas, where Cara's stepfather resides.

Isaiah feels sure that his wounds are healed, his body is strong, and his life's work in the construction field is satisfying. He is positive about his life and future and has immense feelings of gratitude to the people of the town of Ennis. He fondly remembers Amy Cooksey, who he says reached out to him continuously for five years after the 2003 shooting to check up on him in all ways.

"The main thing I remember about the days after the shooting is how this entire town circled around me and let me know that I was not alone and would not be forgotten," Isaiah said. "I know it was the same with all of us. All of the survivors felt the same. I feel honest admiration for the community and how it handled the grief, the loss, and the healing which had to take place after the 2003 Ennis shooting."

## GAVIN FAULKNER

Gavin Faulkner lives in Prescott Valley, Arizona and works for Corbin Electric as a software engineer for a construction company. He is also a gifted writer and will hopefully find time in his life to grow that talent.

In 2018, Gavin entered a three-month rehabilitation program, which led to his current, more than three-year-long, sobriety. He is now involved with Narcotics Anonymous and feels like he has left those lost years behind him. He acknowledges the loss, but with a youthful exuberance, shares that he is looking forward to furthering his career and living a life full of love and peace.

Gavin wrote: "I would never attempt to generalize all tragedies or even this one, as no two people ever experience anything the same. I just hope that by telling my struggle it may help someone with theirs."

## NICOLE TOPPEL GRIBBONS

Nicole resides in Gilbert, Arizona, with her husband, Bryon Gribbons, and their three children. Nicole remains close to her two friends, Ginger Powers Nelson and Angie Hoe Kujula, with whom she spent the most terrifying and haunting night of her life.

"I mostly just want to forget about this event," she said, "and it has taken me a long time to reach that goal." She attributes her recovery to the love of her parents, sister, husband, children, and friends. "I can't stress how important to me the warmth of the community was."

## JASON KLAUMANN

Jason works for Granite Construction and resides in Fruit Heights, Utah. He is married to Beth Toivonen Klaumann, and they have two children.

"I don't think anyone or anything could have changed the outcome of George Davis's carnage, with any different actions," Jason said. He shared that he didn't regret any of his actions in response to the assault and in caring for the victims. He added, "I have had some thoughts considering if the outcome would have been different had I brought my own vehicle into town that night, because I do possess a concealed weapons permit, and I would then have had immediate access to a gun. I now ponder whether that would have had a positive or negative effect, and on balance, I am glad that was not part of the equation."

When community-raised funds were offered to Jason, as they were to other nonwounded though heavily impacted people, he declined. He felt no need for them, being at that time fully employed and self-sufficient. Although he does say that the offer meant a lot to him.

Jason appreciates how Amy Cooksey kept him apprised of all the legal matters, as the case against George Davis proceeded through the various hearings. "Amy was always immediately on the phone to tell me first-hand, what had occurred. I know that mine was the longest statement made in the early morning hours in Sheriff Dave Schenk's vehicle, parked on Main Street. I remember that it took me two hours to write my statement. I know that County Attorney Roberta Zenker's *Information and Belief,* setting out the facts with which to charge Davis, relied heavily on my account."

To this day, Jason would be able to stand on Main Street and show where each shot was fired. He shared that it took a month for his adrenaline to drop to normal. There was a bullet hole in the bottom panel of the door of the Silver Dollar, which bothered Jason for years, and he was very glad when he noticed that it had been changed out. "Unfortunately, I do still suffer from some PTSD from the night of June 14, 2003," he said. "I suffered a bout when I was in a training situation where sirens were going off, and it maybe triggered the memory of the sound of the panic alarm."

He noted another bout of PTSD when his wife came close to attending the music festival in Las Vegas in 2017. "Stephen Paddock shot into the crowds resulting in sixty-one deaths. Just thinking how she could have been there set me back for a few days," he said.

Jason's parents, Martha and Stan Klaumann, spoke of a recent bachelor party that Jason attended. Some of the men were sleeping in a room, which filled with carbon monoxide from a heating system leak. Jason managed to pull all the guests to safety. In that event, as on the night of June 14, 2003, Jason acted with no regard for his own safety, for the benefit of people at risk and in danger. It is his nature. This is the definition of a hero.


## ANGIE HOE KUJULA

Angie resides in Bozeman, Montana with her husband, Levi, and two daughters. She and Levi own and run an online guitar teaching business.

Angie was given time off by her supportive employer, First Security Bank, to attend all the George Davis court hearings. "I had the most peculiar feeling five years ago… I could not get rid of the thought that George Davis could be out of prison on parole," she said. "I had to find out! I couldn't stop thinking about how he could so easily find me, Nicole, and Ginger."

After researching the matter a little, she confirmed for herself that he received an equivalent of a life sentence with no possibility of parole. "Finally, I was comforted," she said. "But that doesn't mean I may not have that feeling again in the future!"

## MATTHEW ORTEGA

Matthew has returned to Ennis, owns a house there, and works with his father and brothers in their family business, the Center Pivot Installation company. They travel a lot and work within a large geographical area.

"I believe that my body is fully recovered, and I feel very blessed," he said. "I know that I will live this life without the benefit of a spleen to fight off infection, and that will just make me very careful whenever I am subjected to an infection or fever."

He is still overwhelmed today at all the support he received from the Ennis community. "There were so many cards written to us, the money raised and the great support for all of those involved," he said. "I also count as a blessing the new friends that I made…that remain true friends to this day, and for that, I am forever grateful."

## GINGER POWERS (NELSON)

Ginger is now married to Kyle Nelson, and they are the managers of Black Mountain Ranch in Ennis. Ginger also works in the office and as a teacher's assistant for the Ennis School District. Her son Cameron is 25 years old. Ginger and Kyle also have two children of their own.

"I still feel the love of this community," she said. "I still am amazed when I remember the food, the money raised for all of us, and the numerous acts of kindness and love which surrounded me and Mike Carroll after the shooting." She feels immense gratitude for the nurses at the Madison Valley Hospital who provided home visits and cared for their wounds. "I'm not sure I ever thanked them enough at that time and I wish I had done so publicly. I hope I can do that now!" Ginger also overflows with appreciation for her family. "My parents, Jim and Marilyn Powers, and my sisters, Susie, Kelly and Cindy and my brother Luke were always there for me," she said. "I will always remember and appreciate them for that."

## TRETT SUTTER

Trett resides in Puyallup, Washington and works for the Washington State Department of Transportation. He is married to Danielle Sutter, and they have two children.

"My memories are primarily of the love and support given to me in the months following the shooting," he said. "I am still in awe when I remember the cash contributions and the people who stopped by to check up on me as I rehabbed afterwards. I am still, to this day, overwhelmed at the warmth of the Town of Ennis and the whole community."

## BEN LINDEMAN, PA-C

Ben Lindeman is married to Jackie Lindeman, and continues to practice medicine in Plains, Montana. Ben's participation in the production of this book was premised on the hope that it would bolster the survivors and the community as a whole, as well as bring peace for the family of Jamie Roberts. He firmly believes that "Ennis as a community should never hang its head in shame for the happenings stemming from one deranged man marauding into the lives of so many, but rather, they should be proud of their capacity to be and do so very much more than most, in their response in the time of tragedy."

Ben now travels to trauma symposiums around the state and at the University of Washington to speak about the impromptu emergency triage that was so necessary after the shooting. Changes to the statewide trauma system occurred due to his feedback after the crisis.

# Epilogue

In the twenty plus years since 2003, many changes have occurred in Ennis and the Madison Valley. Most of the people who moved here did so to enjoy the lifestyle and unmatched vistas afforded by this small town in Montana. Some people who have lived here for decades, or even generations, wonder if its core values and qualities can survive such growth. It is evident to me that they have and will continue to do so.

On a particularly cold late-November night last year, a young couple in Ennis had just given their one-year-old daughter a bath. They were getting her ready for bed when they suddenly smelled smoke. Their toddler girl had left a hanger behind the wood pellet stove and it caught a spark. A molten fire immediately consumed the living room wall. Horrified, they saw the flames spreading throughout their trailer home.

The father rushed his pregnant wife and baby out into the bitter cold, running back into the flames to get their dogs out of an enclosed room. When all were safely outside, shivering and gazing open-mouthed, they watched their home crumple inward as the fire consumed every single possession they owned.

With his family out of harm's way, the father frantically evacuated the surrounding neighbors, including an elderly woman and her pets. The volunteer fire department arrived, and they were able to put out the threatening flames, but not before the entire trailer home was lost. The surrounding homes, however, were safe.

The destroyed house was next door to the Assembly of God Church. The pastor there gave the family immediate shelter. Word went out in every imaginable manner—phone, email, social media, and of course neighbor-to-neighbor. By the next morning, one room of the church spilled over with a mound of clothing, coats and winter gear, baby supplies, toys and books for the child, and kitchen wares. Cars continued to pull into the parking area as countless community members carried in boxes.

The pastor of the church set up a special bank account, and people rushed to donate money. A local woman offered long-term housing for the family and their dogs, and the family had a beautiful Christmas with her and her friends. The owner of Madison Foods set up an additional community fund to benefit them and put the word out via social media. For several weeks, donations continued to flow in for this family.

Even more recently, I saw another outflow of community care. A local woman—a business owner and young mother—was confronted with a long course of cancer treatments for which she would need to travel frequently to Bozeman. The word went out, and her friends, and even women who had yet to make her acquaintance, signed up for a "meal train". The intention of the organizer was clear: to take one worry away from this woman. As is usual in this community, the volunteers quickly outstripped the need, and the train needed "brakes" or this lucky family would have run out of freezer space! The efforts of the participants provided the family with healthy meals continuously throughout her weeks of treatment, along with a dose of loving care.

Also this year, a new expanded Madison Foods replaced its predecessor right next door. The old building is now a locally-owned furniture store. That was a big change for our community, but it was one facilitated by our long-standing, barn-raising ethic. The grocery store owner put out a call for aid on moving day, and a large group of townspeople showed up to assist her with the exciting one-hundred-yard move.

Our medical services have also expanded. The new Madison Valley Hospital was built more than a decade ago, providing the growing community with expanded critical care access. Even that larger facility is now bursting at the seams, and its leadership are planning to expand again in the future.

The Town of Ennis Volunteer Ambulance Service, which existed in 2003, was replaced by the Madison Valley Ambulance Service in May 2021. The community now benefits from a fully staffed ambulance service, which has integrated EMTs and paramedics into the hospital system. There are now two advanced life support ambulances with a third ambulance available. They respond within two minutes to 911 dispatches. These same EMTs and paramedics work in the emergency department as Emergency Room Technicians and assist nursing and medical staff in the hospital, clinic, and throughout the facility.

That was another major change and again, it was characterized by kindness and connection. The town of Ennis and the EMS volunteers generously donated their ambulance and related equipment to the Madison Valley Medical Center during this transition. In 2024, the Madison Valley Ambulance Service won the Montana EMS Service of the Year Award.

As for all the new faces in town, many want to genuinely engage with the community. They do look for ways to connect, meet people, and to actually contribute to the lifestyle that attracted them here. "There is no reason to be bored in Ennis," said town elder Ann Restvedt. She chatted with me years ago, describing the numerous volunteer organizations one can join including The Madison Valley Women's Club, The Ennis Lion's Club, The Madison Valley Rural Fire Department, and The Chamber of Commerce, to name a few. The new Ennis Senior Center provides daily Meals on Wheels and a community gathering point. The Madison Valley Medical Center Foundation provides support to the Madison Valley Medical Center through grant-writing, fundraising, and donor outreach. The Madison Valley Hospital Auxiliary and Madison Valley Manor-Auxiliary provide support and services to employees, patients, and residents of those facilities. There are, in fact, 207 non-profit 501(c)(3) organizations in Madison County. Most have an ongoing need for volunteer involvement.

As I write this in the summer of 2024, I recognize that Ennis and the Madison valley are rapidly changing and growing in population. Burgeoning residential neighborhoods have sprung up inside and along the town limits. Hundreds of people have moved to the valley in the past decade, eager to experience the way of life that still exists here.

It is easy to become bewildered as change and growth occur. It is human nature to resist such change. But in this Montana community, one does not need to look far to find the very same "heart" which existed in 2003. There are only a handful of examples here. There are so many other stories which could be told to show clearly that the heart of this community still beats strongly, and that this is a culture in which love… still wins.

# Acknowledgements

Immediately following the shooting, with Davis' whereabouts still completely unknown, there are certain citizens whose actions rose to the level of heroic: Jason Klaumann, Scott Wright, Jake Stewart, Doug Clark, Nicole Toppel (Gribbons), Angie Hoe (Kujula), Don Schaufler, Laura Clark (Helling), Officer David Clark, Stan Klaumann, Ginger and Andy Guinn, Steve Loucks, Wade Miller, Barbara and Brad Bradshaw, Susie Sprout, Jamie Neiswander, and others. I think of them all as angels living among us. Though none of these individuals would ever describe themselves as heroes, I believe that heroes are simply people who place others' well-being above their own, and act accordingly—when other people in the same situation might become all too aware of the potential danger and act solely (and understandably) to save themselves. By that definition, yes, those named above qualify as heroes! I am grateful to you, and your community thrives today, in gratitude to you. There may be some missing from this list. I apologize! I did my best to find and name everyone.

Most of the survivors and their families shared with me how Amy Cookesey reached out to them repeatedly, not only in the days immediately following the shooting, but for years afterward. She clearly communicated to them that this was the most important case she had ever handled, and their welfare was constantly close to her heart. Amy was and is a passionate advocate. Our community, and our story, would not be the same without her.

Sharon Clark's file was an immeasurably valuable source of written documentation regarding all that transpired during and after the Ennis 2003 shooting. Only a parent would have had the presence of mind during such a tragic time to keep everything. I am deeply grateful for her sharing these resources regarding the most difficult time in her life.

I am also grateful to all the medical personnel who provided interviews and timelines. PA Ben Lindeman's detailed written recollections were a tremendous resource for recreating the timeline of events at the hospital after the shooting. Margaret Bortko, NP was the first person who gave me her recollections for this book. Nurses Jaime Roberts, Jody Sprout, Linda Ryan, and Tana Overcast (Becher) were also invaluable sources as I wrote the medical response scenes.

The survivors themselves provided many interviews that were clearly challenging for them. It is not easy to recall something that you'd much rather forget! I cannot thank them enough. Jason Klaumann's written statement comprised not only the factual basis for the prosecution of George Harold Davis by the State of Montana, but it also served as a highly detailed outline as I crafted the chapter describing the crime itself. Matthew Ortega's e-mail correspondence was so full of reflective detail and memory; it provided a wealth of information for this book. He not only recalled those harsh moments, he also pulled profound life lessons out of that time. I am sure that skill will serve him well his whole life. Gavin Faulkner has kept detailed journals for years. He shared many thoughtfully written recollections regarding the night of the shooting. These resources were immensely helpful. I hope he continues to grow his writing talent. I am also grateful to Ginger Powers (Nelson), Isaiah Crowley, Trett Sutter, Angie Hoe (Kujula) and Nicole Toppel (Gribbons) who allowed me to interview them and provided countless fact-checking details regarding their own personal experiences that night and during the recovery year afterward.

Thank you to Roberta Zenker, the former County Attorney for Madison County, Montana. Her valuable insights and recollections formed the core of the legal reports. Susanne Hill, owner of *The Madisonian*, generously opened the newspaper archives on many occasions. In fact-checking timelines, I benefitted from the reporting of Holly Schmeck (Barney), who wrote for *The Madisonian* at the time of the shooting. Mark Dobie, Publisher of *The Bozeman Daily Chronicle*, generously released key articles written at that time. Nick Gevock, a reporter for *The Bozeman Daily Chronicle*, became a friend of the Ennis community. He had written about our region before, but truly earned our trust for his heartfelt and humane coverage of this trying time.

A community of established writers and editors equipped me to take the first steps into writing this book and cultivating my writing life. I am deeply grateful to Montana screenwriter, playwright, actor, and teacher Allyson Adams; her writer's workshop truly sparked to life the writer within me. Thank you to Ginger Holdeman, my forever writing partner, and best example of a writer's work ethic I could ever hope to meet. Andrea Davis, a friend for most of my life and a literacy advocate, provided many thoughtful and helpful comments. Fellow Ennis writer and author Kitty Donich (aka Katherine Leigh) has been a friend for over 40 years and empowered me by sharing her perspectives as a published author. Anika Hanisch, of Montana Coauthor, was the greatest content editor, line editor, and friend throughout the years this took me to write. She taught me how to corral a tremendous volume of research and various perspectives into a cohesive book. She exhibited great patience and professionalism with me when I most needed it. I am forever grateful for that.

My author-support community grew even more when it was time to share the manuscript with a larger pool of beta readers. Some were already good friends, others I've never met. I'm immensely grateful to you all. Sherry J. Scott, a long-time friend and role model, provided several supportive comments and helpful notes. Professional editor Ingrid Nemzek shared many supportive insights and last-minute editorial remarks, for which I am most grateful. I've heard she would like to meet the Ortega family and Amy Cooksey; I understand why. Thank you to Simeon Morell. I was so honored that this young police officer, balancing a career and a family, would take the time to read and provide valuable insights. K. Shimkin also read a semi-final draft and gave invaluable critique, drawing from her EMS experience and therapeutic training.

Thank you to my twin sister, Karol Gans, for reading countless versions of this book with her teacher's attention to detail. Your positive and valuable support never waivers, and it sustains my core being. Thank you to my children, Duncan McMullin, Morgan McMullin, Courtney McMullin, and Conor McMullin for connecting me to the community of Ennis through all their friends and activities. Having four adult children doing so well in this world as wondrous spouses, parents, and citizens gives me continuous peace of mind. Finally, thank you to my husband, Paul, for simply understanding that "I had to write this book." The radiant contentment of our life together allowed me the time I needed to complete this.

44701407-5191-4bc3-9cbf-cebafbb6c3eaR03

Made in the USA
Las Vegas, NV
13 October 2024